———— →»»«««← ————

This Edition is printed from type and
is limited to Three Hundred Copies.

No.————————

———— →»»«««← ————

HISTORY OF THE

Court of Common Pleas

OF THE

CITY AND COUNTY OF NEW YORK

WITH

FULL REPORTS OF ALL

IMPORTANT PROCEEDINGS

— BY —

JAMES WILTON BROOKS, LL.D.

OF THE NEW YORK BAR

NEW YORK
PUBLISHED BY SUBSCRIPTION
1896

D. K. F.

COPYRIGHT 1896
BY
JAMES WILTON BROOKS

PRESS OF WERNER, SANFORD & CO., 108 EAST 16TH STREET, NEW YORK.

PREFACE.

During 1895 the writer contributed a number of articles to the New York press. One of these entitled "End of the Common Pleas," was published in the *Sun* of May 19th. This book is the sequence of that article. It is not a law treatise. The decisions of no Court have been better reported than those of the Court of Common Pleas of the City and County of New York. It treats of the personal side of the Court, and is in a measure, therefore, supplementary to the Reports. The writer may have erred in dealing so little with the many interesting trials, decisions and questions of law which have arisen and have been adjudicated during the life of this Court. He has been frequently tempted also to include such stories and anecdotes as have come within his knowledge, and they have been many, but has refrained because he wished rather to produce a work which should be dignified and in keeping with the spirit of one of the oldest, if not the oldest, Court our people have known.

The "Minutes" are gone into at some length, because the proceedings covered by them are historical, and for the reason that this part of the history of the Court has nowhere else been printed.

Sketches of all, and portraits of twenty-one of the twenty-three Judges identified with the later history of the Court, will be found within these covers. There are also portraits of many whose names appear in the text. Without the peculiar experiences incident to the collecting of biographical data, there can be no conception of the amount of labor involved. The simple note in the appendix concerning Judge Inglis gives little or no idea of the amount of time and inquiry devoted to obtaining the material for his sketch, and yet scarce half a century has passed since he sat on the bench.

The author wishes to gratefully acknowledge the great assistance rendered to him by Chief Justice Joseph F. Daly and by the Associate Judges of the Court. His grateful acknowledgments are due to the former Chief Justice Charles P. Daly, to Judges George C. Barrett, George L. Ingraham, Frederick W. Loew, George M. Van Hoesen, to Mr. Nathaniel Jarvis, Jr., and to the relatives of several of the Judges of the Court. Their aid has enabled him to obtain data not otherwise available, and this is especially true in regard to the biographies of those who are gone. He takes this opportunity also to particularly thank his friend, Mr. James E. Homans, for his help in the arranging of manuscript and reading of proofs, and for many suggestions of value. Most of the portraits have been drawn especially for this volume by Mr. B. F. Williamson, and others are reproduced through the courtesy of the publishers of the "National Cyclopædia of American Biography."

The work which the Court has accomplished has now become a matter of history. The future alone will determine whether the action of the people, through their delegates in the Constitutional Convention of 1894, and subsequently at the polls, was wise or unwise. The change has been brought about, so to speak, not from the bottom up, but from the top downward. No popular demand was heard. The necessity of relieving the New York Court of Appeals from its enormous pressure of work was the cause of the consolidation of the superior local Courts with the Supreme Court. The immediate result is the increased number of Judges and the formation of the Appellate Divisions of the Supreme Court, which not only hold the authority of the former General Terms, but by reason of the finality of their decisions will be possessed of great public significance.

JAMES WILTON BROOKS.

New York, July 1st. 1896.

6

CONTENTS.

THE COURT OF COMMON PLEAS DURING THE DUTCH DOMINATION.

THE Court of Common Pleas, founded in 1686, in the City of New York, extended in 1691 throughout the State, restricted again in 1846 to the City of New York, and finally in accordance with the amended State Constitution of 1894, passing out of existence on the thirty-first of December, 1895, was the oldest judicial tribunal in the State of New York. It succeeded "The Worshipful Court of the Schout, Burgomasters and Schepens," which was established in 1653, and may thus be said to have had a continuous existence of nearly two centuries and a half. It was twice as old as the nation. In its passing away may be seen the severance of one of the last links which bound our present to the old days when the language of our city was Dutch, when its Courts were Dutch, and when its law came straight from Holland.

Though the Court of Common Pleas of the City and County of New York was not established till towards the end of the seventeenth century, the prior judicial history of the State of New York is well worth a summary.

No provision seems to have been made for several years for the administration of justice in the colony established by the West India Company in 1623, on Manhattan Island. Presently, however, in 1626, Peter

9

Minuit, the first Governor, surrounded himself with a council of five, which became invested with all powers, judicial, legislative and executive. An official, well known in Holland as the "Schout," was attached to this body.

The Governor, the Schout and the Council were subject to the supervision and appellate jurisdiction of the authorities at Amsterdam.

The Council continued to administer justice during the official tenure of Minuit and of his successor, Van Twiller, a period of eleven years. Its records have been lost.

Whatever were the duties of the Governor and his Council of Five, there can be little doubt but that almost everything conceivable, except judicial decision, was entrusted to the "Schout Fiscal." He combined in himself the power of a public prosecutor and the executive duties of a sheriff. He was far more than either or both these functionaries according to any current understanding. It was his duty, under the orders of the Governor's Council, to arrest and arraign in behalf of the Company all persons accused of crime; to superintend the trial and see to the proper carrying out of the sentence.

Such was the unbiased nature of this primitive Court, however, that the Schout must note all evidence for as well as against the prisoner, and see to it that no facts were suppressed on either side. He was also required to keep a strict account of all information taken by him, and of all criminal trials, and regularly transmit reports to the Company's main offices in Holland. And his duties were further framed so as to make him the protector and custodian of all prisoners, whom he was obliged at the earliest opportunity, to bring to trial. Prisoners, whether innocent or guilty, were not to be allowed to languish in jail.

His duties further obliged him to act as chief of police, or general constable, in seeing to the execution of all placards, ordinances, resolutions and regulations of the States General, as well in Court as out of it.

In some towns of Holland the Schout was the chief officer of the Board of Burgomasters. He convoked all Courts, but took no further part in the proceedings except to count the votes. Nor had he any voice in the deliberations, unless as public prosecutor, when he was obliged to leave the bench to the senior burgomaster. He was an officer somewhat analogous to the speaker of our legislative assemblies, or the moderator of the "town meeting" in the good old days.

In 1630 Patroon Courts were established, local Courts where the Patroon exercised within his territory unlimited civil and criminal jurisdiction. The Patroon had even power of life and death. His decisions, however, within certain limits, were subject to an appeal to the Governor of New Amsterdam.

Thus matters went on with more or less variation until the impetuous, hot-tempered but forceful Peter Stuyvesant came as governor in 1647. Immediately on his arrival he established a Court of Justice whose jurisdiction was certainly broad enough, for it was empowered to decide "all cases whatsoever," subject only to the mild restriction of practically referring everything of any importance to the governor for his approval. Popular discontent with this tribunal grew apace, and out of the wrangle between the governor and the colonists, which brought about a number of trips to Holland, covered a number of years and abounded in dramatic incidents, grew "The Worshipful Court of the Schout, Burgomaster and Schepens." This tribunal consisted of the Schout, four Burgomasters and nine Schepens.

The Burgomasters took turns among themselves, each for a term of three months to attend at the City Hall for the despatch of public business. Their office, like that of the Schout, was mainly administrative. The duties of the Schepens were entirely judicial, having jurisdiction of both civil and criminal causes. The three orders of officers, however, formed a "College," and enacted the laws and ordinances for the city somewhat, likely, after the "General Court" of the Colony of Massachusetts, and were known as a body under the title of the "Lords of the Court of the City of New Amsterdam." Such a "College" was presided over by the Schout in the old country, but in New Amsterdam, either a president duly chosen or the senior Burgomaster assumed the dignity.

It seems really remarkable that so complicated and imposing an institution should have been deemed essential for the relatively small and insignificant City of New Amsterdam. Nevertheless, this body was really an instrument of peace rather than of strife.

If to-day an action is brought before our judiciary, it is fought as it were inch by inch by the opposing counsel. The judgment when obtained, is enforced to the uttermost farthing. The cause may go to a referee, but his duties are simply those as it were of an umpire. Nor does our law make any account of the defendant,

P. Stuyvesant

Cadwallader Colden

Jas Duane

John Jay

unless the defendant looks out for himself. It was different in old New Amsterdam; the Court was of so Arcadian a character, so utterly pledged to the eccentric notion that all men are somehow brothers, or if not that they ought to be, that it was loath to exercise its judicial authority; to enforce the execution of justice. It was a Court of conciliation, a begetter of harmony, which from its very pomposity and ceremonialism was all the more potent as authority to compel the resumption of friendly relations. If a cause were brought before it, each party stated his case to the best of his ability and then the judges rendered their decision on the facts, or appointed arbitrators to bring the opponents together. These arbitrators were appointed to review the matter thoroughly and agree upon some basis of compromise which was usually accepted by both parties. Says Chief Justice Charles P. Daly, in his History of the Judicial Tribunals of New York, from 1623 to 1846 : "It is worthy of remark that though the amount involved was frequently considerable, appeals to the Court from the decision of the arbitrators were exceedingly rare. Indeed, the first appeal to be found upon the records was brought by a stranger."

If, however, the opponents differed in their version of facts, they were put under oath to testify, and if the discrepancy still remained, witnesses were called in, affidavits presented or depositions taken, which were duly presented on the next court day.

The defendant was also, like the female sex with the English common law, the especial "favorite" of the Court. Court was held at least every two weeks, and frequently every week. When the case was first entered an officer known as the Court Messenger, at the request of the one aggrieved, verbally summoned the defendant to appear at the next court day. If the defendant failed to appear he lost the right to make any objection to the jurisdiction of the Court, and incurred the cost of the summons. Failing to appear on the first court day thereafter, he was again summoned; when, failing to appear, he incurred additional costs, lost the right to apply for adjournments or delays, or to make any " dilatory exceptions" whatsoever. But the Court was still long-suffering, and like an affectionate parent of a phenominally prodigal child, again summoned, and besought him to look after his own personal interests; although in failing for the third time to heed the kindly admonitions, he lost all power of appeal and all right to review the case. Yet if the Court really believed his presence essential to his own well-being, as well as to the good name of justice in the colony, a fourth citation might be issued in the nature of an arrest, and he be " haled" before the august assemblage and compelled to defend himself.

It was customary to appear on the first citation. If the matter involved was intricate, or it was difficult to get at the truth, it was the practice to refer the matter to arbitrators, who were always instructed to bring about a reconciliation if they could. These references were frequent upon every court day and, in fact, the chief business of the Tribunal was in acting as a Court of Conciliation.

Then the arbitrators went to work, but if no reconciliation could be effected, the case was again brought to Court by the dissatisfied party and the final decision was made. When judgment was rendered for a sum of money, time was given for payment, usually fourteen days for the discharge of one-half, and the remainder to be paid within a month. If at the expiration of the time the debtor had not paid, the Schout, or more often the Court Messenger, went to him, exhibited a copy of the sentence and also his wand of office, which was a bunch of thorns, and summoned him to settle the matter within twenty-four hours. If the debt was not liquidated, a second visit was made, still another twenty-four hours were allowed, and then at the expiration of the forty-eight hours, the delinquent's movable goods were seized and after an allotted time, six days, were sold at public auction.

Greater formalities were required in the sale of real estate. The manner of selling was peculiar. The officer lighted a candle; the bidding went on while it was burning; he who had offered the most at the extinction of the candle was the purchaser.

The Dutch law, though on the whole infinitely superior to the more technical and artificial system introduced by their English successors, was a kind of irregular mosaic, and it is not surprising that the Governor and his Burgomaster and his Schout and his Schepens were continually in hot water.

THE ENGLISH PERIOD.

In 1664 the Colony passed into the hands of the English, and while the gradual development of the legal procedure during the period from 1664 to the date of the Charter, which takes its name from Governor Dongan and which was granted to the City of New York in 1686, is extremely interesting, the merest statement of facts will suffice.

Established in the City of New York in 1686, a Court of Common Pleas was created in each county throughout the State by the Act of 1691. The judges and clerks were in general, appointed by the Governor, and held office during his pleasure or so long as their own behavior was good.

The Court had cognizance in all actions, real, personal and mixed, where the amount involved exceeded five English pounds. Its errors were corrected in the first instance, by the Supreme Court, to which appeals were allowed for any judgment where the amount involved exceeded the sum of twenty English pounds, or about one hundred dollars of our money.

The Court of Common Pleas in the City of New York was known for many years, in fact until 1821, under its original Dutch name, and was called "The Mayor's Court." Its criminal branch was known as "The Court of Sessions."

Until the end of the Dutch domination, and even long

afterward, the governors of the colony counted it a right to preside in Court and to order the affairs of justice, and this was a particular embarrassment of the cause, not only because they knew no law, but also because some of them seem to have been fitter subjects for its discriminations than interpreters of its principles. Indeed, most of them were adventurers, pure and simple; men whose careers had been "unfortunate" on the other side, and who had come to the New World to begin again.

In addition to their salary, the governors claimed and received a large income in fees or perquisites for arranging patents or grants in land, and, on account of this malfeasance the Crown was constantly defrauded, while they, its servants, set worthy examples to the ring-politicians of later generations. Yet while their understanding of the law was extremely "liberal," there was always fear of that dreadful bogey the "reformer," who might some day disturb the peace of the colonists and instigate proceedings in the name of the Crown to void the grants thus fraudulently made. This fear was the real upshot of the almost frantic opposition of the colonists to the establishment of the Court of Chancery, or any court of equity whatsoever, for had some wealthy Knickerbocker been sued to make a test case, it is probable that the majority would speedily have found themselves *sans* house, *sans* land, *sans* patent, *sans* everything; and there had been fewer vast fortunes to accrue from New York real estate holdings.

This then was a bond of sympathy and common cause between the colonists and their often rascally governors, which rendered the former only too thankful to bear any forms of tyranny rather than the dread assizes of the Court of Chancery. None the less, the Court came, remaining during many generations; and as the colonists had evidently feared, the governors too often filled the office of Chancellor.

Some of the colonial governors had the honesty to acknowledge their ignorance of the law and behave accordingly. Thus John Montgomerie, who became governor in 1728, positively declined to sit, and when ordered to do so on the authority of the Crown, acquiesced with all unwillingness, encouraging the learned counsel on either side by informing them that he knew nothing whatever of law, but would be pleased to hear them talk and might "patch up" a decision sooner or later. As a matter of fact, he gave but one decree and issued but three orders, with the help of his counsel; and died in 1731. He was followed by several persons who either from their great learning or intense ignorance, even of ignorance itself, rushed in where their predecessors had feared to tread and rendered decisions at haphazard, sometimes to the consternation of the worthy counsellors and occasionally to the "vindication of the persecuted."

So matters continued with more or less regularity until Sir Charles Hardy became governor in 1755. Hardy had been a seaman by profession, and having been knighted for some service or other to the mother country, was sent to New York Colony to enjoy his laurels in quiet. He was informed on arriving that it was necessary for him as governor to sit in chancery; and having heretofore overcome many difficulties, was nothing daunted, and sat. But his honest heart was sorely tried by the broadside of demurrers launched at him by four learned counsellors. "Gentlemen," he cried, "my knowledge relates to the sea; that is my sphere. If you want to know when the wind and tide will suit for going to Sandy Hook, I can tell you; but what can the captain of a ship know about demurrers? If you dispute about a fact I can look into the depositions and perhaps tell you who has the best of it; but I know nothing of your points of law."

Hardy later tried to hear a case of fact only, but failed so signally that he called in the three justices of the Supreme Court to assist him; and thereafter they discharged the duties of Chancellor for him.

One of the governors of New York, Sir Henry Moore Bart, who was appointed executive in 1765, unfortunately died in 1769, leaving a number of patents unexecuted to the total value in commissions of something like 10,000 pounds. None more thoroughly appreciated the opportunity than Cadwallader Colden, who had through several administrations exercised the office of lieutenant-governor and was conversant with the "duties" of the executive office. He at once assumed the duties of governor *pro tem.* With pertinacious industry he worked literally night and day on the matter and had finally issued the last patent.

The succeeding governor, John Murray, further known by the title of Lord Dunmore, straightway he landed in his realm, made formal demand on Colden for "a moiety or one half part" of all fees, perquisites and emoluments that had accrued during his year as acting governor, and was of course refused.

Dunmore, however, was a man of ready expedients,

and friendly persuasion having failed, proceeded to institute proceedings against his lieutenant after the most approved burlesque fashion. He ordered the attorney general to file a bill against Colden in the Court of Chancery where the governor was sole judge, and directed that it should be in the name of the Crown.

Colden, nevertheless, was not at all intimidated by these drastic measures, but deliberately set about employing counsel to plead his case. He found an attorney, by name James Duane, subsequently a judge, who was sufficiently emancipated from the current awe and dread of those in authority, and a good lawyer for that day when good lawyers were apparently few, to argue his case. At the day of the trial Lord Dunmore took his seat in the capacity of Chancellor and despite that Duane showed conclusively in his argument that the suit could not be maintained, would allow nothing, not even legal principles to thwart the "rights of the Crown." The attorney-general and his colleague, Smith, the historian of the Court, argued so ably on the other side as to impress the worthy Colden most unfavorably. He is quoted as saying of Smith, that he displayed "an easiness of principles that enabled him to affirm, deny or pervert anything, with a degree of confidence that might deceive the unwary."

Even Dunmore seemed to have considered that his (the Crown's) case had been argued too well—been over-argued, in fact—and in spite of his inclination to reward the talents of Smith, found himself unexpectedly faced with the unquestioned principles of law and equity. He pretended to consider the case one of such moment as to require some little review and consideration, appointing the following Thursday for the rendering of his decision. Thursday came, and the matter was adjourned a fortnight. Meanwhile, he and his advisers busily consulted law and precedent, but in vain. Then doubtless in confidence of his official prestige the cause was referred to the four judges of the Supreme Court. They presently unanimously decided that Duane's demurrer was well taken and that the suit could not be maintained.

LATER HISTORY OF THE COURT.

The Mayor's Court was continued through the Colonial Period. The City records leave it in doubt as to whether the Court was or was not held during the War of the Revolution.

In the beginning of 1784 James Duane was appointed Mayor, and from that time on, there is no break in the sittings of this Court. Mr. Duane, a lawyer by profession, who as we have seen defended Cadwallader Colden in the attack made upon him by Lord Dunmore, had acqured a large practice before the Revolution, and during that period had served as a member of the Provincial Congress and as a delegate to the Continental Congress. His high character drew into his Court every lawyer of ability. The leading practitioners were, for instance, Alexander Hamilton, Aaron Burr, Col. Troup, Edward Livingston, Brockholst Livingston (the latter afterwards Judge of the Supreme Court of New York, and from 1806 until 1823 one of the Judiciary of the United States Supreme Court), Egbert Benson, Morgan Lewis and Josiah Ogden Hoffman, the father of Ogden Hoffman, who was Attorney General from 1795 to 1802, and Associate Justice of the New York Supreme Court from its creation until his death, men whose first forensic effort was made in the Mayor's Court.

Judge Duane presided till the close of 1789 when he was appointed by Washington United States District Court Judge.

Morgan Lewis.

DeWitt Clinton

John Jay

Edw. Livingston

By the Dongan Charter it was provided, among other matters, that the Mayor, the Recorder and Aldermen, or any three of them, of whom either the Mayor or Recorder were required to be one, were authorized to hold the Mayor's Court, or the *Court of Common Pleas.* It was presided over by the Mayor and Recorder alternately.

During the following thirty years and more, 1789 to to 1821, the list of Mayors and Recorders who sat in this Court included many of the most distinguished lawyers of the State. The Mayors were: Richard Varick, Edward Livingston, De Witt Clinton, Marinus Willet, Jacob Radcliffe and Cadwallader D. Colden ; and the Recorders were : Samuel Jones (father of the late Chief Justice), James Kent, Richard Harrison, John B. Provoost, Maturin Livingston, Pierre C. Van Wyck, Josiah Ogden Hoffman, Peter A. Jay and Richard Riker.

While Maturin Livingston was Recorder, Mayor Clinton ceased, perhaps from choice, perhaps from lack of time, to preside in the Mayor's Court, and from that time on the Recorder sat as presiding judge until 1821, when from the fact that its business had greatly increased, and that the Mayor had ceased to preside in it, it was concluded that the name Mayor's Court, no longer in any sense appropriate, should be abandoned. An act was prepared by John Anthon, then the most prominent practitioner at the bar, and was passed by the Legislature, changing the name to the " Court of Common Pleas of the City of New York," and the office of " First Judge " was created. The Governor appointed John T. Irving as First Judge. The Mayor, Recorder and Aldermen were

23

still authorized to sit in Court as formerly, but the First Judge was empowered to hold it without them, and it was his special duty to hold it. The leading practitioners before him were : John Anthon, Martin S. Wilkins, Elisha W. King, John T. Mulligan, Robert Bogardus, Pierre C. Van Wyck, Thomas Phoenix, Joseph D. Fay, David Graham, Sr., Hugh Maxwell, John Leveridge and Wm. M. Price, though the members of what was then known as the senior bar. Thos. Addis Emmett, Peter A. Jay, Peter W. Radcliffe, Sam M. Hopkins, David B. Ogden, Wm. Slosson, Wm. Sampson and others appeared frequently in the Court as associate counsel in important cases.

In 1834 an Associate Judge was provided. He was vested with all the powers of the First Judge. The Governor appointed Michael Ulshoeffer. His standing both at the bar and in the community is best shown by the fact that he had already served the people as City Attorney, Corporation Counsel, and as member of Assembly, and that he had been in turn a vestryman of St. Mark's and of Grace churches, two of the most influential congregations in the City of New York. On the death of Judge Irving, in 1838, Judge Ulshoeffer was appointed First Judge, which office he held till his retirement in 1848, and Daniel P. Ingraham (the father of Judge George L. Ingraham, now a Justice of our Supreme Court), was appointed Associate Judge.

Meanwhile (1839) the business of the Court increased so rapidly that an additional judge, vested with all the powers of the other judges, was created, and William Inglis was appointed as an Associate Judge— thus making the full bench of The Common Pleas consist of three judges. The number was increased to six in 1870.

In 1844 Chas. P. Daly, then only 27 years of age, was appointed in the place of Judge Inglis.

The Constitution of 1846 especially excepted from the general Judicial reorganization of the State, the Court of Common Pleas and the Superior Court of the City of New York.

A law enacted in 1847 provided, however, that the judges of both Courts should be elected by the people.

All the existing judges (Ulshoeffer, Daly and Ingraham) of the Common Pleas were elected in June, 1847. The allotment of their judicial terms, for, in accordance with the provisions of the law, each took his chances in drawing by lot, resulted in Judge Ulshoeffer's securing the two-year, Judge Ingraham the four-year and Judge Daly the six-year term.

In 1849 Lewis B. Woodruff was elected in place of Judge Ulshoeffer; and in 1850 Judge Ingraham was chosen First Judge. Judge Ingraham was re-elected in 1851, as was also, in 1853, Judge Daly.

Their successors were: John R. Brady (1856–1869), Henry Hilton (1858–1863), Albert Cardozo (1863–1868); Hooper C. Van Vorst (1867–68); Geo. C. Barrett (1868–69); Frederick W. Loew (1869–75); Charles H. Van Brunt (1870–84); Hamilton W. Robinson (1870–79); Richard L. Larremore (1870–90); George M. Van Hoesen (1876–90); Henry Wilder Allen (1884–91), and Joseph F. Daly (1870–96); Miles Beach (1879–96); Henry W. Bookstaver (1885–96); Henry Bischoff (1890–96); Roger A. Pryor (1890–96); Leonard A.

Giegerich (1891–96), who constituted the last Bench of the Court of Common Pleas.

There have been since 1821 but twenty-three judges, four of whom served as "First Judges," and three, Judge Chas. P. Daly, Judge Larremore and Judge Joseph F. Daly, as "Chief Justices."

Two have died before the expiration of their term. Judge Robinson in 1879 and Judge Allen in 1891. Judge Allen was stricken in the Court House as he was leaving his Court, and died a few days afterwards in the hospital.

The following table will show the succession of Judges together with the dates of their elevation to the Bench:

COURT OF COMMON PLEAS, NEW YORK.

SUCCESSION OF JUDGES.

Year	First Judge	Associate Judge	Additional Associate	Robinson	J. F. Daly	Larremore
1821	Irving.	First Judge under the Act of 1821, when the Court was changed from the Mayor's Court to the Court of Common Pleas.				
1822						
1823						
1824						
1825						
1826						
1827						
1828						
1829						
1830						
1831						
1832						
1833						
1834		Ulshoeffer Associate Judge, created by Act of 1834.				
1835						
1836						
1837						
1838	Ingraham.					
1839			Inglis. Additional Associate; Act of 1839.			
1840						
1841						
1842						
1843						
1844			C P. Daly.			
1845						
1846						
1847						
1848						
1849		Woodruff.				
1850						
1851						
1852						
1853						
1854						
1855						
1856		Brady.				
1857						
1858	Hilton.					
1859						
1860						
1861						
1862						
1863	Cardozo.					
1864						
1865						
1866				Three Additional Judges created by the CONSTITUTION of 1869.		
1867	Van Vorst.					
1868	Barrett.	Loew.				
1869						
1870	Van Brunt.			Robinson	J. F. Daly	Larremore
1871						
1872						
1873						
1874						
1875		Van Hoesen				
1876						
1877						
1878						
1879				Beach.		
1880						
1881						
1882						
1883						
1884	Allen.					
1885			Bookstaver			
1886						
1887						
1888						
1889						
1890		Bischoff.				Pryor.
1891	Giegerich.					
1892						
1893						
1894						
1895						

LENGTH OF SERVICE OF EACH JUDGE OF THE COURT OF
COMMON PLEAS.

Charles P. Daly ....41 years.
*Joseph F. Daly..25   "
D. P. Ingraham..20   "
R. L. Larremore 20   "
John T. Irving...17   "
M. Ulshoeffer...16   "
*Miles Beach..16   "
**Charles H. Van Brunt..14   "
George M. Van Hoesen...14   "
John R. Brady...13   "
*H. W. Bookstaver 11   "
H. W. Robinson... 9   "
Fred. W. Loew.. 7   "
Henry W. Allen... 7   "
L. B. Woodruff 6   "
*Henry Bischoff, Jr.. 6   "
*Roger A. Pryor.. 6   "
William Inglis... 5   "
Henry Hilton... 5   "
Albert Cardozo... 5   "
*L. A. Giegerich... 5   "
H. C. Van Vorst.. 1   "
*** George C. Barrett.. 1   "

---

*Still on the Bench; transferred to the Supreme Court by the Constitu-
tion of 1894.

**Still on the Bench; elected to the Supreme Court in 1883.

***Still on the Bench; elected to the Supreme Court in 1871.

Judge Larremore resigned on account of illness with
eight years of his term unfilled and Judge Charles P.
Daly was retired on account of age at the expiration of
his sixth consecutive term of judicial office.

The Court has been noted from the fact that its
justices have, with rare exceptions, been eminent
jurists, and that every noted advocate in the City of
New York has appeared at its bar.

The original roll of the Court from 1821 to 1848,
during which period every aspirant to the Bar of the
City of New York had first to be admitted to practice
in the Common Pleas, shows almost every New York
name which was prominent at that period, whether in
the legal, social or business world. In those days every

would-be lawyer had to pass several examinations before he was admitted to full practice.

He was first admitted to the Common Pleas as attorney at law. After three years of active practice he applied for admittance as counsellor at law to the Supreme Court. He had also to pass a special and supposedly equally thorough examination in the Court of Chancery.

This original roll contains the names of those admitted to practice law, the dates of their admittance to practice, and the oaths to which they were compelled to subscribe. The first was of course the usual oath to support the Constitution, and uphold the dignity of the Court.

And then came an oath indicative of the times, but of interest at any period, the duelling oath, which reads as follows:

I, ——————, do Solemnly Swear that I have not been engaged in a Duel by sending or accepting a Challenge to fight a Duel, or by Fighting a Duel, or in any other manner in violation of the act entitled " An Act to Suppress Duelling " since the first day of July in the year of our Lord one thousand eight hundred and sixteen, nor will I be so concerned directly or indirectly in any duel during the continuance of the said Act and while an Inhabitant of this State.

The roll includes the names of men who became eminent as lawyers, judges or statesmen, with the year of their admittance to practice.*

Among these occur, in 1823, Thomas L. Wells, Samuel Verplanck, Abraham Ogden, Jr., William Betts.

*As the original roll of the Court is far too long for publication in this volume, a selected list is here given of such names as have appeared most prominent or familiar.

In the year 1824 appear the names of Judge William Kent and Philip Hamilton and D. P. Ingraham, afterwards Judge of the Court of Common Pleas.

In 1825 appears the names of William Inglis, afterwards Judge of the Court of Common Pleas; Francis Griffin and Gen. John A. Dix, afterwards Governor of New York, and F. Brockholst Cutting, and E. C. Benedict.

In 1826, N. Bowditch Blunt, afterwards District Attorney, and Judge Thomas S. Brady, the father of John R. and James T. Brady; Philo T. Ruggles and Charles Edwards.

In 1827, D. Graham, Jr., Pierre M. Irving, Charles A. Clinton and Judge T. W. Clerke, and Daniel B. Talmadge.

In 1828, Judge Benjamin W. Bonney, Edward Sandford and David Dudley Field.

In 1829, A. D. Russell, Judge John A. Lott, John McKeon, afterwards District Attorney, and Benjamin D. Silliman, who is at this writing the oldest graduate of Yale College, and one of the oldest living members of the New York Bar.

In 1830, Robert H. Morris, afterwards Mayor, Recorder and Judge; Robert R. Lansing, Peter Wilson and Hamilton Fish, afterwards Governor of New York, U. S. Senator and U. S. Secretary of State.

In 1831, Edgar S. Van Winkle and Judge Henry E. Davies, the father of Julian T. and William G. Davies, both well-known members of the living bar.

In 1832, Alexander Hamilton and Corporation Counsel Robert J. Dillon.

In 1833, Albon P. Mann, Judge Henry P. Edwards

30

and John T. Irving, Jr., and Thomas A. Brady, brother of John R. and James T. Brady, and Henry C. Murphy.

In 1834, Judge William Minot Mitchell and Nelson Chase.

In 1835, James T. Brady, Theodore Sedgwick, Judge William H. Leonard and Judge Gilbert M. Speir, C. J. DeWitt and Edward DeWitt.

In 1836, Judge Joseph S. Bosworth, Judge Claudius L. Monell and Andrew Warner, who was afterwards one of the four clerks of the Court of Common Pleas, and is now, at the age of ninety, the president of the Institute for Savings of Merchant Clerks.

In 1837, Horace F. Clark, Luther R. Marsh, Hiram Barney, Augustus Schell and Charles E. Butler.

In 1838, John Jay, John W. C. Leveridge, Judge John W. Edwards, William C. Noyes and Benjamin F. Butler, the father of William Allen Butler, the leader of our elder bar, and grandfather of William Allen Butler, Jr., the president of the Lawyers' Club of the City of New York.

In 1839, Chas. P. Daly, for many years Judge, First Judge and Chief Justice of the Court of Common Pleas, and Vice-Chancellor Lewis H. Sandford.

In 1840, Recorder James M. Smith, Jr., Judge Charles A. Peabody and William J. Hoppin, for many years secretary of our legation to Great Britain and Edward W. Stoughton.

In 1841, John Riker and Henry L. Riker.

In 1842, William T. Horn, John R. Brady, afterwards Judge of the Court of Common Pleas and of the Supreme Court; Nelson J. Waterbury, afterwards District Attorney, and Judge Enoch L. Fancher.

In 1843, John E. Burrill.

In 1844, Judge Charles A. Rapallo, Samuel J. Tilden, afterwards Governor of the State of New York; John E. Devlin and Charles Price.

In 1845, William C. Barrett, Judge Abraham B. Tappen, Judge Ogden Hoffman, Jr., John J. Townsend and Henry A. Cram.

In 1846, Andrew H. Green, Henry Hilton, afterwards Judge of the Court of Common Pleas; Judge Henry P. McGown, James W. Gerard, Jr., and Henry Morrison.

As the Court of Common Pleas was the County Court of New York County, it had exclusive jurisdiction in certain actions.

It was the Court of Impeachment for municipal and minor judicial officers. Until within a few years it was the only Court having jurisdiction in cases of forfeited recognizances, or in cases where bonds when confiscated became the property of the City Treasury. Until recently it was the only Court which could give an individual the legal right to change his name.

The greater part of lunacy proceedings, mechanic lien litigations and insolvent assignments came before the Court of Common Pleas. It was also the Court where contested wills were tried before a jury. Its equity powers were co-equal with those of the Supreme Court. In connection with the Supreme and Superior Courts, nearly all of the naturalization of the county was done in it—only a small percentage of certificates being issued by the United States Court. Its appellate powers were more varied than those of any New York Court excepting the Court of Appeals.

32

Peter Augustus Jay

R. Riker

B. F. Butler

W. A. Duer

The Supreme Court heard only appeals from its own and from the Surrogate's Court. The Superior Court was confined to appeals from its own decisions. The Common Pleas, in addition to the appeals from its own decisions, passed in review on appeal, such judgments of the City Court and the District Courts of New York as were appealed. There are six judges of the City Court and eleven District Court Judges. Legislation is often inaugurated in the lower courts which keenly affect the general public. As the decisions on appeal of the Common Pleas were final it determined the law, so far as these lower courts were concerned, on all matters presenting questions not distinctly adjudicated by the court of last resort.

The first suits in the Elevated Railway cases were brought in this Court. The foreclosure of the little spur built by the first believers in the elevated system, which ran along 9th avenue, through that part of the city known as Chelsea, near the Episcopal Theological Seminary, was brought in the Common Pleas.

Until near the end of its existence the Common Pleas was the only Court where one might apply for an "order" or permission to change one's name.

Its reports show no end of queer wishes in this respect. One gentleman goes at great length to state his objection to his own and, in fact, to all names, and wishes to be allowed to change his name to the letter "A." That the matter was not to be laughed at is shown by a long opinion by the Chief Justice denying the application.

From 1821 to 1854 the Clerk of New York County acted as Clerk of both the Supreme Court and of the

Court of Common Pleas. In 1854 an act was passed creating a clerk of the Court of Common Pleas to be appointed by the Judges of the Court. The Judges selected Andrew Warner, who served one year. He was succeeded by Benjamin H. Jarvis, who served one year, and from then to 1896, when the Court passed out of existence, there were only three clerks, Nathaniel Jarvis, Jr., Samuel Jones and Alfred Wagstaff, and all were members of the New York Bar.

Mr. Warner is to-day the President of the Institution for the Savings of Merchants' Clerks. Mr. Jarvis, after serving for over a third of a century, resigned in 1889. Judge Jones, coming of a family of lawyers, several of whom were on the Bench, retired in 1892. Senator Wagstaff, who served as Clerk from 1892 to 1896, is now the Clerk for the Appellate Division of the Supreme Court for the First Judicial District of New York.

On the walls of what was the General Term room in the Court House, may yet be seen the portraits of Judge Ulshoeffer, Robinson, Brady, Daniel P. Ingraham* and Charles P. Daly. The adjoining room contains an alto relievo of Judge Irving and a bust of Thomas Addis Emmett. The inscription on the latter tells that Mr. Emmett died "among these benches, within these official walls." A bust of Alexander Hamilton adorns the furthermost corner.

The decisions of the Common Pleas since 1850 have been reported in twenty-three volumes, four of which have been edited by E. Delafield Smith, two by Judge

---

* The portraits of Judges Brady and Ingraham have, since Jan. 1st, 1896, been removed to the rooms of the Appellate Division of the Supreme Court.

Hilton and sixteen by Chief Justice Charles P. Daly. In addition to these, known respectively as E. D. Smith's Reports, Hilton's Reports, and Daly's Reports, other decisions are to be found in the voluminous Abbott's Reports (both series and new cases), Howard's Practice Reports, The New York State Reporter, The New York Supplement, The Miscellaneous Reports, The Civil Procedure Reports, The Weekly Digest, The Law Bulletin, and The New York Transcript, The Daily Law Register and The New York Law Journal, the last three being successively the daily official papers of the county.

A RESUME OF THE MINUTES OF THE COURT OF COMMON PLEAS OF THE CITY AND COUNTY OF NEW YORK SITTING AS A COUNTY COURT FOR SPECIAL PURPOSES.

THE book of minutes of proceedings by the Judges of the Court of Common Pleas, outside of their ordinary judicial functions, commences with an entry of June 2d, 1832, recording their appointment of a District Attorney according to the power then vested in them. The Court at that time consisted of John T. Irving, First Judge; Walter Bowne, Mayor; Richard Riker, Recorder; and the Aldermen of the city, and they re-appointed Ogden Hoffman, the then incumbent of the office.

IMPEACHMENT OF DAVID M. COWDREY.

The Court convened again on January 26th, 1833, to try David M. Cowdrey, Clerk to one of the Assistant Justices of the city, for official misconduct. On the second day appointed for the hearing of the charges there were present John T. Irving, First Judge; and Aldermen Cebra, Sharpe, Ferris, Rhinelander, Meigs, John Palmer, James Palmer, Mandeville, Woodruff and Murray. A quorum being present the Court proceeded with the trial. Justice Eber Wheaton, the prosecutor, was represented by Charles O'Conor as counsel, and the accused, David M. Cowdrey, by Francis B. Cut-

W. L. Marcy.

Wm C. Bouck

Hamilton Fish

John A. Dix

ting. The trial occupied seven days. Witnesses were examined and the Court, having advised in the matter, after due deliberation, removed Cowdrey from his office.

APPOINTMENTS FOR DISTRICT ATTORNEY.

The Court was next convened on May 22d, 1835, to appoint a District Attorney. The First Judge, the Recorder and ten Aldermen were present(Labagh, Taylor, Benson, Lamb, Delamater, Purdy, Fickett, Varian, Lovett and Nixon), and Thomas Phoenix was appointed.

The next appointment of District Attorney was made June 4th, 1838, Daniel P. Ingraham being Associate Judge, Aaron Clarke, Mayor, Robert H. Morris, Recorder and Benson, Thomas, Lynch and Thomas G. Talmadge, Aldermen. James R. Whiting was appointed.

TRIAL OF JUSTICE JOHN M. BLOODGOOD.

On February 19th, 1839, the Court was convened to try John M. Bloodgood, one of the Special Justices of the city, upon charges. Michael Ulshoeffer was then First Judge, Daniel P. Ingraham, Associate. The Recorder, the Mayor and fourteen Aldermen were present. George F. Talman appeared as counsel for the prosecution, while Charles O'Conor, Francis B. Cutting and John A. Morrill appeared for the accused. The charges were dismissed for want of verification by oath, and as deficient in specifications sufficient to authorize the Court to proceed thereon.

TRIAL OF JUSTICE HENRY W. MERRITT.

The next official tried before the Court was Henry W. Merritt, a Special Justice, and the Court convened

37

for the purpose on April 1st, 1840, with Judges Ulshoeffer, Ingraham and Inglis, the Mayor, the Recorder and twelve Aldermen present. The District Attorney, James R. Whiting, appeared for the prosecution and Francis B. Cutting and Charles O'Conor for the accused. Mr. Cutting objected to the charges as not in due form. The Court adjourned to consider the question and subsequently decided that the charges were sufficiently authenticated to put the accused upon his defense. The vote upon this decision was as follows: In favor of sustaining the charges, the Recorder, Judge Inglis and seven Aldermen. Against the sufficiency of the charges, Judges Ulshoeffer and Ingraham and three Aldermen. The trial was ordered to proceed on April 7th, but upon that day Mr. O'Conor filed a plea to the jurisdiction of the Court and the matter was adjourned to April 8th, when the plea was overruled. The accused then filed a challenge to the competency of the Mayor and of the Aldermen of the city to proceed or act as judges of the Court in the hearing of the matter. The challenge was overruled. Whereupon the accused filed a demurrer to the charges. The demurrer was argued at length by Mr. Cutting, the District Attorney, Mr. Whiting and Mr. O'Conor, and the demurrer was sustained by the Court with leave to the District Attorney to renew the charges amended and verified, and for that purpose the Court resolved to assemble on the 11th of April. On that date charges and specifications were again presented by the District Attorney against Justice Merritt and he was required to answer. He was represented by the same counsel, who renewed their motion to set aside the pleadings for irregularity, their

38

plea to the jurisdiction and their challenge to the competency of the Mayor and Aldermen to act as judges, all being overruled. The accused then filed exceptions to the first and second charges and pleaded not guilty to the third charge. Judgment was given in his favor to his demurrer to the first charge. Argument was then heard upon the demurrer to the second charge and this consumed three days, ending in the demurrer being overruled, one Judge and four Aldermen voting to sustain the demurrer and one Judge and six Aldermen to overrule it. Judge Ingraham not having heard the arguments on the demurrer to the second charge did not vote. The trial of the issue upon the third charge, to which the accused had pleaded not guilty, was then proceeded with and consumed eleven days, eighty-one witnesses being sworn and examined. The cause was then summed up, Mr. O'Conor occupying seven and one-half hours in his address, Mr Cutting four and one-half hours, and the District Attorney three and one-half hours of one day and the whole of the next. The Court was adjourned on account of the illness of the Recorder, and from time to time until June 9th, 1840, when judgment was rendered acquitting the accused on the second charge, the Recorder and two Aldermen being in favor of a verdict of guilty, and the three Judges and two Aldermen voting for not guilty. As to the third charge, of which there were three specifications, the Court was divided on the first and second specifications, the Recorder and three Aldermen voting for guilty and the three Judges and one Alderman voting not guilty. As to the third specification, there was one vote for guilty by Alderman Nash, and seven votes for not guilty by

39

the three Judges, the Recorder and three Aldermen, and the decision was that the Court being thus divided in opinion the charges be dismissed.

JAMES R. WHITING APPOINTED DISTRICT ATTORNEY.

The Court convened on May 17th, 1841, to appoint a District Attorney, their choice falling upon James R. Whiting, he receiving on the first ballot thirteen votes, and on division being called for, nineteen votes out of twenty-four.

A PROTEST.

A protest against the right of Associate Justices of the General Sessions to sit in the Court, signed by eleven of the Aldermen, was presented, and a motion was made to enter it upon the minutes, which was lost.

TRIAL OF JUSTICE MILN PARKER.

On August 7th, 1841, the Court was convened to try Miln Parker, a Special Justice, upon charges and specifications. The charges presented by Isaac J. Wood, through Abraham D. Russell, as counsel, were ordered to be served on the accused and delivered to the District Attorney, and the Clerk was directed to notify the Judges of the County Court to attend on the 7th of September. On the last named day the Court met, the Aldermen sitting as members. George M. Van Cott appeared as counsel for Justice Parker and was granted until the 11th inst. to plead to the charges. The District Attorney, on motion of counsel for the prosecutor, was requested to assist in conducting the prosecution. On the adjourned day the Court assembled, the District

Attorney appearing with the attorney for the prosecution, and Horace Holden, James T. Brady and D. M. Van Cott appearing as counsel on behalf of the accused. The trial occupied nine days and twenty witnesses were examined. Edward Sanford appeared on the third day as associate counsel for the prosecution. The summing up occupied two days. Written opinions were delivered by Judge Ingraham and the Recorder in favor of the acquittal of the accused and the Court, consisting of the three Judges of the Common Pleas, the Recorder and fourteen Aldermen, unanimously dismissed the charges, all the members voting in the affirmative.

TRIAL OF JUSTICE WILLIAM WILEY.

On January 10th, 1842, the County Court met to consider a communication received from the Mayor enclosing a certificate of the Clerk of the Court of Oyer and Terminer, showing that William Wiley, one of the Assistant Justices of the city, had been convicted of receiving stolen goods with knowledge. The Court requested the District Attorney to make charges against the Justice "in order to his removal from office, unless the necessity of such removal is dispensed with by the resignation of said Justice being accepted by the Common Council." On the adjourned day, January 14th, 1842, the District Attorney appeared and Alderman Campbell made a motion that inasmuch as Justice Wiley had tendered his resignation to the Common Council and it was in the power of that body to accept it, the Court should adjourn in order that that body might act on the same. The motion was lost. The District Attorney then made the charges against the Justice which were ordered on file. A copy was directed to be served on him with notice to appear on the 3d of February following, when it having been communicated to the Court that the Common Council had accepted the resignation of the Justice and had appointed a successor, it was ordered that further proceedings be discontinued.

QUESTION OF INCLUDING NAMES OF ASSOCIATE JUDGES.

On July 26th, 1842, the Court (as the County Court of New York) convened to consider the question whether the names of the Associate Judges of the General Sessions should be entered on the minutes of the Court as Judges thereof. The Mayor objected. The Recorder moved that Judge Lynch be heard in support of the motion. Judge Lynch made an argument in favor of the motion and was followed by the Mayor in opposition. Judge Inglis moved that the resolution lie on the table to enable the members of the Court to examine the subject, and the Court adjourned to the first Monday in September. The Mayor requested the mover to withdraw his motion, which being complied with, he asked for what precise purpose an order had been made in the Common Pleas convening the Court. Judge Inglis replied that the order had been made pursuant to written requests signed by three of the Judges in behalf of the thirteen judges of the Court without stating the object. An adjournment was taken to July 27th, and on that day Alderman Davies read an opinion in favor of sustaining the claims of the Associate Justices of the General Sessions to sit as Judges of the County Court. Judge Ingraham delivered an adverse opinion in which Judge Inglis concurred. The Recorder gave an opinion sustaining the right of the Associate Justices, and the First Judge (Ulshoeffer) delivered a written opinion adverse to the claims of the said Judges to sit as Judges of the County Court generally, but in favor of the call of the names of said Judges whenever matters relating to the appointment of a District Attorney was agitated. A vote was taken on the question before the Court, which resulted in a tie. The matter was then laid on the table and the Court adjourned *sine die*.

TRIAL OF JUSTICES GEORGE W. MATZEL, MILN PARKER AND EPHRAIM STEVENS.

On September 8th, 1842, the Court met to consider a presentment of the grand jury sent by the General Sessions to the First Judge of the Common Pleas in relation to the conduct of certain Special Justices. The Court, on motion, adopted an order proposed by Judge Ingraham referring the presentment of the grand jury to counsel (Matthew C. Paterson) for the purpose of examining into the charges therein preferred against the Special Justices and if sufficient evidence could be secured to sustain such charges before the Court that he be directed to prepare charges for such purpose and report the same to the Court. On September 23d, 1842, the Court having assembled, Mr. Paterson presented a report prepared pursuant to the foregoing order, accompanied with charges and specifications against George W. Matzel, Miln Parker and Ephraim Stevens, Special Justices, and an order was made requiring the accused to answer on the 4th day of October and copies of the charges and specifications were directed to be

43

served upon them. On the return day Matthew C. Paterson appeared in support of the charges, and Messrs. Brady, Lord and Price appeared for the Justices. Mr. Paterson read an affidavit of Floyd Smith as to the truth of the charges, which was filed. An affidavit of the service of the charges and a copy of the rule to answer upon the Justices was filed. Mr. Paterson called upon the accused Justices to answer or plead to the charges. Mr. Brady, on behalf of the Justices, objected to answer or plead to the charges in their present form, charging the Justices jointly for separate and specific acts done by them, and suggested that the prosecutor amend them instanter and they would then be ready to answer and proceed to trial at once. Mr. Paterson contended that the charges were properly prepared and that the Justices should plead to them in their present form. To this Mr. Lord objected and stated that unless they were amended a motion must be made to quash them. After hearing further argument, the Court, through the Recorder and the three Judges of the Common Pleas, considered the charges defective for the reasons suggested by the counsel for the Justices, and an order was made permitting the prosecutor to change the accusations so as to charge the several Justices separately, and that the charges so amended be printed and served four days before the meeting of the Court. On the 18th of October the Court convened and Mr. Paterson tendered to the accused the charges against them as amended. Their counsel objected on the ground that they were entitled to four days' service of the same, which objection the Court sustained. An adjournment

44

Marinus Willett

[signature]

[signature]

John McKe [signature]

was had until the 25th inst. Messrs. Paterson and O'Conor then appeared for the prosecution, and Messrs. Brady, Lord, Price and Holden for the Justices. An objection was made on their behalf that the charges were not substantially the same as those directed by the Court to be amended, and that the new charges, if entertained, were not sufficiently verified. This motion was argued, and on a subsequent day the Court rendered its decision denying the motion to quash but amending the charges so as to strike out the names of certain Aldermen contained therein, and all reference to said Aldermen, and adding the words "divers other persons," names of the confederates as charged, and directing the defendants to answer. Pleas of not guilty were put in by the Justices and filed on the next day, and the Court took an adjournment to November 2d, when the trial commenced. Two witnesses duly subpœnaed were attached for non-appearance. The charges against each Justice were separately heard. The trial of Miln Parker occupied fourteen days and the charges were finally dismissed; all the Judges and thirteen Aldermen voting for acquittal and three Aldermen voting for conviction, and it was then recommended by the Court to the counsel acting on behalf of the prosecution that all further proceedings against the other Justices, Matzel and Stevens, be discontinued unless some new evidence which might adduce a conviction exist in those cases, and Mr. Paterson having stated that he had no new evidence to offer against the last named Justices, it was ordered that the charges against them be also dismissed.

45

TRIAL OF DR. C. H. JACKSON.

On March 2d, 1843, the Court assembled to try a charge preferred by the New York County Medical Society against Dr. Charles H. Jackson. The full bench was present, together with fourteen Aldermen. The charge was sustained.

RESIGNATION OF DISTRICT ATTORNEY JAMES R. WHITING.

On the 29th of May, 1843, the Court assembled to receive the resignation of James R. Whiting as District Attorney. On motion the letter was engrossed at length on the minutes of the Court. It was as follows:

NEW YORK, May 11th, 1843.

DEAR SIR:

I hereby resign the office of District Attorney for the City and County of New York. I respectfully ask you to communicate it to the Honorable Court over which you preside at your earliest convenience. As no fit occasion has presented itself since my appointment of tendering my thanks to the Court for their partiality in selecting me to fill so important an office, I have deemed it now not unfit to return to them my warm acknowledgments for the high honor conferred upon me. I accepted the trust with thankfulness, and have to the best of my ability performed its functions. I part with it without regret, but with a lively sense of gratitude to the appointing power, cheered by the consciousness which I think I may, without presumption, entertain, that I restore the trust unsullied by any act of mine. I will continue to perform the duties of the office until it shall please the Court to supply the vacancy, and in the meantime have the honor to be, with great respect,

Your obedient and humble servant,

J. R. WHITING.

HON. MICHAEL ULSHOEFFER,
First Judge of the County Court, City of New York.

On June 19th following the Court assembled to consider the resignation. An adjournment was had to June 28th, 1843, when the Court resolved that it deemed it inexpedient to accept the resignation of James R. Whiting as District Attorney.

COMPLAINTS PREFERRED.

At the same meeting the Mayor stated that a complaint had been preferred against Justice Gilbert by Henry Smith, John C. Jackson and James Gerry, and that he was requested to present the same to the Court. On motion, it was resolved that the same be referred to a committee of three Judges of the Court to examine and report thereon. The following Judges were appointed as the said committee: Aldermen Woodhull, Tillon and Brevoort. On February 28th the Mayor handed in the charges exhibited against Justice Gilbert by Andrew McGown. These charges were referred to the same committee. At the next meeting of the Court, March 4th, 1844, the First Judge of the Common Pleas stated that he had convened the Court to present a petition of James Moncrief preferring a complaint against James B. Greenman, Clerk to the Assistant Justice of the Fifth District Court. This petition was referred to the same committee. On March 12th, 1844, the Court convened. Alderman Woodhull, of the committee to whom the complaint against James B. Greenman was referred, presented a written report recommending that further proceedings in the case be discontinued. The report was accepted.

The First Judge presented a complaint of Josiah M. Foote against Ebenezer Stevens, a Special Justice, which was read and referred to Alderman Woodhull's committee.

On March 26th, 1844, the Court met, and Alderman Woodhull reported in favor of dismissing the complaint of Josiah M. Foote against Justice Stevens. The report was adopted.

The same committee reported on the complaint of Andrew McGown against Justice Gilbert. On motion, it was ordered that charges be preferred against Justice Gilbert. The vote upon the motion was eleven in the affirmative, including Judges Ingraham and Inglis and nine Aldermen; and eight in the negative, including Judge Ulshoeffer and seven Aldermen. It was ordered that the District Attorney prepare the charges to be founded upon the complaint presented to the Court. On May 6th, 1844, the Court met to proceed with the hearing of the charges. On this occasion Judge Charles P. Daly sat for the first time in the Court. The District Attorney, Mr. Whiting, appeared for the prosecution, and David Graham, Jr. for the defendant, who, being called upon to plead to the charges, pleaded not guilty. The evidence upon the charges was taken before the Court on several days, down to and including May 11th, 1844, and eleven witnesses were examined. The case was summed up and submitted, and, the Court having re-convened, Alderman Scoles and the First Judge read written opinions. On motion, the Court proceeded to consider each specification separately. It was decided that "the first specification of the first charge is proved except as to the *quo animo* therein charged." The vote

48

Thos. Addis Emmet

Ch. O'Conor

John K. Porter

stood eleven to nine, Judge Daly, Recorder Talmadge and ten Aldermen voting in the affirmative, and Judges Ulshoeffer, Ingraham and seven Aldermen in the negative. It was decided that " the second specification of the first charge except as to the *quo animo* is proved " by a vote of fourteen to seven. A similar decision was made as to the third specification of the first charge by a vote of twelve to nine. A similar disposition was made as to the fourth specification of the first charge by a vote of eighteen to three, all the Judges, the Recorder and fourteen Aldermen voting in the affirmative and three Aldermen in the negative. It was decided " that the fifth specification of the first charge and that the sixth specification of the first charge was not proved." On vote being taken on the first charge, Justice Gilbert was declared not guilty, by a vote of eight to thirteen, all the Judges and the Recorder voting in the negative. The vote on the second charge was taken generally, and he was declared not guilty by a vote of two to nineteen, and the following resolutions submitted by the First Judge were adopted:

First. *Resolved*, That although the evidence in the case of the articles of impeachment against Justice Gilbert does not justify the arrest, detention and commitment of Mr. McGown as a disorderly person, nor the fine hastily and summarily and without an adjournment imposed upon Mr. Lewis by said Justice, and although the conduct of the Justice does not meet with the approbation of this Court, still it appears by the evidence that the errors committed by the Justice may have been errors of judgment and were not the result of malice, corruption or oppression.

Second. *Resolved*, therefore, That the charges against

49

Justice Gilbert are not substantiated in such a manner as to justify his removal from office, and that consequently he stands discharged therefrom.

These resolutions were adopted by a vote of twelve to nine, all the Judges and the Recorder, with eight Aldermen, voting in favor of, and nine Aldermen against them.

MR. MATTHEW C. PATERSON APPOINTED DISTRICT ATTORNEY.

On June 10th, 1844, the Court met to appoint a District Attorney in place of Mr. Whiting, from whom the First Judge read a letter calling attention to the fact that his term of office expired on the 4th inst. Matthew C. Paterson was appointed to succeed him, the vote standing thirteen in his favor, three for William Inglis (ex-Judge of the Court of Common Pleas), and two scattering.

COMPLAINTS AGAINST JUSTICES JOSEPH HASKELL AND WILLIAM WALN DRINKER.

On Tuesday, January 21st, 1845, the Court convened at the request of the Mayor for the purpose of receiving certain complaints against the official conduct of Joseph Haskell and William Waln Drinker, Special Justices.

The Court convened again on February 11th, 1845, when Alderman Schieffelin made a motion that the District Attorney be authorized to associate with himself additional counsel to aid in conducting the proceedings. The motion was opposed by Judge Ingraham on the ground that it was a matter discretionary with the

District Attorney and contrary to the practice of the
Court; but, the question being taken on the motion, it
was adopted, and the District Attorney then stated that
he had associated Ogden Hoffman as counsel, who
appeared and took his seat. The District Attorney
filed the charges and specifications against Justices
Haskell and Drinker and called upon Justice Haskell
to plead. George Wood and James T. Brady appeared
as counsel for Justice Haskell, and Mr. Brady before
he proposed to plead to the charges made a motion to
strike out the fifth charge and addressed the Court in
support of the motion. Messrs. Hoffmann and Paterson, respectively, addressed the Court in opposition,
and were followed by Mr. Wood in support of the
motion. A question being taken upon striking out, it
was decided adversely. The answer of Justice Haskell,
pleading not guilty, was then filed, and evidence was
produced. The Court adjourned to the 13th of February, when further evidence was taken. Mr. Brady
called upon the District Attorney to exhaust the testimony on the part of the prosecution of each witness
upon all the charges before he proceeded to their cross-
examination. The District Attorney objected to this,
and stated that he proposed to examine all the witnesses upon each charge and thus dispose of each
charge separately instead of eliciting all the facts within
the knowledge of each witness at once in relation to the
various charges. The counsel for the respective
parties being heard in support and opposition of the
proposed course and a vote being taken thereon, the
course of the District Attorney was sustained by a vote
of ten to eight. Mr. Brady then declined to cross-ex-

amine the witness produced on the part of the prosecution until the direct examination was concluded on all charges. This course was assented to by the District Attorney. Evidence was taken upon that and nine subsequent days, until March 22d, 1845, when the cause was summed up.

At the final meeting there were present the three Judges, Ulshoeffer, Ingraham and Daly, of the Court of Common Pleas; James Harper, Mayor; Frederick A. Talmadge, Recorder, and the following Alderman: William S. Miller, William Gale, William B. Cousins, Lucius G. Drake, William Tucker, Horatio Mott, Jeremiah J. Dickinson, David S. Jackson, Thomas Winship, Stephen Hasbrouck, Richard L. Schieffelin, William C. Seaman and Charles Devoe. Judges Ulshoeffer, Ingraham and Daly, and Aldermen Miller, Dickinson, Schieffelin and Devoe read written opinions of the case; the Mayor and Aldermen Hasbrouck and Gale delivered oral opinions. Alderman Schieffelin offered a resolution that Justice Haskell be removed from the office of Special Justice for the following causes:

1st. Because he has been guilty of arbitrary, oppressive and illegal conduct in the exercises of the duties thereof.

2nd. Because he has been guilty of wilful and malicious conduct in the exercise of his office.

3rd. Because he has been guilty of wilful and gross violations of the duty of a magistrate in conduct tending to defeat the ends of public justice.

4th. Because he has exhibited a violent, ungovernable and oppressive temper, rendering him unfit for the

R. E. Fenton

Orm D. Morgan

L. Robinson

G. C. Verplanck

proper, fair and impartial discharge of the duties of his said office.

Alderman Gale stated that although he was in favor of the removal of Justice Haskell, yet he could not vote for the resolution offered if it contained all the causes assigned for such removal; whereupon Alderman Miller moved that it be amended by striking out the words "wilful and" in the third clause, which was agreed to by a vote of eight to six. The resolution was then adopted by a vote of eleven to seven; the Mayor and ten Aldermen in the affirmative, the three Judges, the Recorder and three Aldermen in the negative. He was, however, acquitted of the first two causes by a vote of eight to ten, and convicted of the last two by a vote of eleven to seven. The consideration of the charges against Justice Drinker was set down for the 9th of April.

On April 9th an adjournment was taken to April 24th.

TRIAL OF JUSTICE DRINKER.

On the 24th of April the Court proceeded to the hearing of the charges against Justice Drinker. Mr. David Graham, Jr., on behalf of Justice Drinker, filed a written answer pleading not guilty to the first and second charges and demurring to the third. A motion being made to strike out the words "has from time to time discharged persons accused of felonies and misdemeanors without examination or bail," in the specification to the third charge, the same were ordered to be stricken out. The demurrer being overruled, the Justice pleaded not guilty to the third charge. Witnesses were called and examined on that and five following days, when the cause was submitted upon the address of counsel and the First Judge and Alderman Schieffelin read written opinions, the Mayor, the Recorder, Judge Daly and Aldermen Miller, Cousins, Drake, Dickinson and Hasbrouck delivering oral opinions.

Alderman Schieffelin offered a resolution that

WHEREAS, The charges against the Justice have in the opinion of the Court been sustained, that he be removed from office for the following causes.

1st. That the said William W. Drinker since his appointment has been guilty of wilful, corrupt and illegal conduct in the exercise of his official duties.

2d. That he corruptly took moneys found in the possession of a prisoner which had been stolen, and appropriated same to his own private purposes.

3d. That he has exhibited want of capacity, either through ignorance or incapacity, to discharge the duties of his said office.

A motion was made that the resolution be amended by striking out the second cause assigned, which was agreed to without a division. Motion was made that the words "wilful, corrupt and " in the first cause be stricken out, which was also agreed to without a division. The question was then put on adopting the resolution as amended and it was decided in the negative by a vote of six to eight, Aldermen Williams and Bunting declined voting, not having heard the whole of the testimony or the argument of counsel.

Judge Ulshoeffer then offered the following resolutions:

1st. *Resolved,* That although this Court strongly

disapprove of the conduct of Mr. Drinker in the respects stated in the charges against him they do not think that he should be dismissed from his office or has been proved to be guilty of corrupt or malicious proceedings in his official duties.

2d. *Resolved* therefore, That the charges against Justice Drinker be and the same are hereby dismissed.

Debate being had thereon, the resolutions were lost by a vote of four to ten. Alderman Miller then moved that the rejection of the resolutions offered by Alderman Schieffelin be reconsidered, which was done by nine affirmative votes. Alderman Miller then moved the adoption of the resolutions of Alderman Schieffelin, which was lost by a tie vote.

Alderman Schieffelin then offered the following resolutions:

Resolved, That although this Court disapprove of the conduct of Mr. Drinker in the respects stated in the charges against him they do not think that he should be dismissed from his office or has been proved to be guilty of corrupt or malicious proceedings in his official duties although meriting the strongest censure of the Court.

Resolved, therefore, That the charges against Justice Drinker be and the same are hereby dismissed.

These resolutions were adopted by a vote of nine to five.

MR. JOHN MC KEON APPOINTED DISTRICT ATTORNEY.

On February 6th, 1846, the Court met to appoint a District Attorney and selected John McKeon for that office.

On April 20th, 1846, the Court met and the First Judge stated that it was convened pursuant to a resolution of the Board of Supervisors for the purpose of investigating the official - conduct of William Waln Drinker, a Special Justice; whereupon, on motion of Alderman Jackson, it was ordered "that the charges be referred to the District Attorney for examination and if sufficient evidence can be procured to sustain the charges, that the District Attorney be directed to prepare charges for such purpose and report the same to this Court."

On April 25th, 1846, the District Attorney presented charges to the Court, and on May 4th appeared in behalf of the prosecution and Lorenzo B. Shepard appeared as counsel for Justice Drinker. A motion to strike out the fourth charge was made by him and he addressed the Court in support thereof, which was denied. The Justice then pleaded not guilty to the charges and specifications, and the Court adjourned on the 13th of May, on which day John McKeon, the District Attorney, and Jonas B. Phillips, Assistant District Attorney, appeared in behalf of the prosecution; Lorenzo B. Shepard and James R. Whiting appeared as counsel for Justice Drinker; Andrew H. Mickle, Mayor of the City, sitting as Judge.

On the 19th of May the Court met (John B. Scott being Recorder) and evidence was taken upon the charges. The trial was continued to and including the 26th of September, 1846, the Court meeting upon sev-

Edwards Pierrepont

James C. Spencer

Henry Day

Thomas McElrath

entccn days between those dates for the examination of witnesses. Charles O'Conor was selected by the District Attorney to assist in the prosecution.

On the 26th of September the Court met and resolved " that although this Court do not approve of many of the official acts of Justice Drinker as called in question by the charges and specifications against him, yet we do not find that sufficient has been proved to call for or justify his removal from office." This resolution, offered by Alderman Benson and seconded by Alderman Stoneall, was adopted by a vote of eleven to seven, and the charges were dismissed.

INQUIRY INTO THE SANITY OF JOHN B. HASTY.

On Monday, December 21st, 1846, the Court convened for the purpose of inquiring into the alleged insanity of John B. Hasty, one of the police clerks of the Special Justices, and into his capacity and competency to exercise the duties of his office. After several adjournments, it was moved that the charges against Mr. Hasty be dismissed, a sufficient time not having elapsed since the alleged insanity to justify his removal from office. This motion was adopted.

TRIAL OF JUSTICE DUFFY.

The Court of Common Pleas as a Court of Impeachment was convened on the 12th of November, 1877, with the following Judges present: Charles P. Daly, Charles H. Van Brunt, Hamilton W. Robinson, Richard L.. Larremore, Joseph F. Daly, and George M. Van Hoesen, the full number of Judges under the amended Constitution of 1869. The Mayor, Recorder, and

Aldermen, having ceased to sit as Judges of the County Court or the Court of Common Pleas since the amended Constitution of 1846, and three additional Judges of the Court having been elected pursuant to the amendment of 1869, Chief Justice Daly presented and filed affidavits and charges made against Patrick G. Duffy, Police Justice, pursuant to an Act of the Legislature of the State of New York, passed May 17th 1873, entitled, "An Act to secure better administration in the Police Courts in the City of New York." The charges and specifications against Justice Duffy were printed and filed in the Court, together with his answer submitted on January 22d, 1878, by Algernon S. Sullivan and Wheeler H. Peckham, his counsel. On the last named day the Court assembled to receive the said answer and Chief Justice Daly then announced that as the several Judges of the Court were at this time so engaged in the different branches of the Court that it would be necessary to postpone the hearing of the testimony until the first Monday of February next, so that all the Judges could attend, and that the Court would adjourn until that day at 11 o'clock, A.M., which was done.

On February 4th, 1878, the Court met pursuant to adjournment, all the Judges except Judge Van Brunt being present. B. H. Phelps, District Attorney, appeared for the prosecution, and Messrs. Sullivan and Peckham for the defence. Witnesses were examined on that and the two following days, when the case was closed on both sides. By the direction of the Court it was decided that the Court proceed to a vote upon the charges and that each charge be heard by the Court and the question be taken guilty or not guilty. The clerk then read charge first, and upon calling each Judge all the Judges voted not guilty. The clerk then read charge second, and upon calling each Judge, all the Judges voted not guilty. Chief Justice Daly then assigned his reasons for his vote, in which all the Judges concurred, and the Court adjourned.

TRIAL OF JUSTICE DIVVER.

On November 23d, 1894, the Judges of the Court of Common Pleas were convened to consider written allegations filed by William H. Hale, an attorney, in behalf of six residents and tax-payers of the city, charging Patrick Divver, a Police Justice, with various offences.

There were present Hon. Joseph F. Daly, Chief Justice, and Judges Henry W. Bookstaver, Henry Bischoff, Jr., Roger A. Pryor and Leonard A. Giegerich.

William H. Hale appeared for the residents and tax-payers; and Daniel G. Rollins and Abraham Levy for the defendant. District Attorney Col. John R. Fellows subsequently appeared for the people.

Adjournments were taken to the 17th, to the 19th, and 21st insts., and on Friday, December 28th, 1894, the Court of Common Pleas sat for the last time as a Court of Impeachment. All the Judges excepting Judge Beach were present.

After listening to the examination of witnesses and the argument of counsel, the Judges, in accordance with the statute, voted publicly upon the charges.

The charges against Justice Divver were in substance:

59

First: That he was habitually careless, negligent and inefficient in the discharge of the duties of his office.

Second: That on or about October 17th, 1894, he had made a violent assault upon one Morris Tekulsky.

Third: That on or about November 3d, 1893, he had instigated persons by the offer of valuable rewards and the promise of positions, to vote the Democratic ticket.

Fourth: That during the year of 1886, he was accustomed to divide with one Edward Parmely Jones, the proceeds of a system of swindling commonly called the " Green-goods Game."

Fifth (supplemental): That he had at various times and places "systematically and habitually conducted and abetted false and fraudulent registration, illegal voting, and frauds in election returns."

The fourth charge had been dismissed upon demurrer, the majority of the Court holding that it alleged misconduct not occurring during the defendant's incumbency of office, and therefore afforded no ground for removal; and, upon the polling by the clerk, each of the five Judges in turn voted either "not proven" or "not guilty" to the first, second, third and fifth charges.

After the polling of the Judges, on motion of the counsel for Justice Divver, the proceedings were dismissed.

JOHN TREAT IRVING.

THE HONORABLE JOHN TREAT IRVING.

John Treat Irving, first Judge of the Court of Common Pleas, was born in New York City, May 26th, 1778, in the quaint, gabled house his father had erected on Vandewater Street.

His father, William Irving, was a native of Kirkwall, the capital of the Orkney Islands, and of good lineage. He followed the calling of a navigator, and for many years sailed on vessels engaged in trade between the ports of New York and Falmouth, England. In Falmouth, he met and married Sarah Sanders, a woman of rare beauty and charm of character, and two years later, in 1763, finally settled in New York City, where he established himself in trade on William Street, midway between Fulton and John Streets.

He was a man of great decision, of a stern type of piety and sense of duty almost puritanic, and exerted a strong disciplinary influence over his sons. During the Revolution his fervid patriotism exposed him to numerous dangers and difficulties, and at one time he was compelled to take refuge in New Jersey.

His son John, like his other brothers, was sent to private schools in the neighborhood of his home—for the city was small then and thinly settled—and was admitted to Columbia College.

Being graduated in 1798, he immediately took up the study of law, in which his marked natural ability and devoted hard work soon gained him a conspicuous position. He was also active in public affairs and during 1816-17 was a member of the State Assembly.

Appointed in 1821 a Judge of the Court of Common Pleas, he served as First Judge, both in title and in chronological order, till his death in 1838, in all seventeen years.

He was possessed of literary ability, and in his earlier years contributed extensively to the columns of the *Chronicle*, edited by his brother, Washington Irving, gaining considerable reputation by his poetical attacks on political opponents. The claims of his profession, however, occupied his time and attention in later years.

From 1818 until his death he was a trustee of Columbia. He was a regular attendant, and for many years a vestryman, of Trinity Church, New York.

In his personal character he was of unflinching integrity and great refinement. He enjoyed the respect of the community and was a recognized leader in public affairs.

Judge Irving's wife was Abby Furman, daughter of Gabriel and Sarah (Wall) Furman, whom he married April 28th, 1806.

Judge Irving died at his home, 37 Chambers Street, New York, March, 15th, 1838. Upon his death a marble tablet with his bust, *in relievo*, and a suitable inscription was placed in the Court room.

His son, John Treat Irving, his grandson, the son of John Treat Irving, Cortlandt Irving, are to-day practicing members of the bar. Another son, Mr. George Irving, acted as one of the secretaries on the occasion

LEWIS B. WOODRUFF, LL.D.

of the final proceedings of the Court on December 30th, 1895.

In his introduction to the first of E. D. Smith's Reports, Chief Justice Charles P. Daly says of Judge Irving: " As a Judge, he was in many respects a model for imitation. To the strictest integrity and a strong love of justice he united the most exact and methodical habits of business. Attentive, careful, and painstaking, few Judges in this State ever have been more accurate, or perhaps more generally correct in their decisions.

"While presiding at *nisi prius*, he was not what would be termed a quick-minded man; but when questions were argued before him *in banc*, he bestowed so much care and considered each case so attentively that his judgments were rarely reversed, and were uniformly treated by the Courts of Revision with the greatest respect."

THE HONORABLE MICHAEL ULSHOEFFER.

Michael Ulshoeffer, second Judge of the Court of Common Pleas, was born in New York City, March 30, 1793.

His father, George Ulshoeffer, born in 1748, at Creglingen, in the dominion of the Margrave of Anspach and Bayreuth, was forced into the British service and sent to America in 1777. Many of these Hessians became in the end citizens of the Republic.

George Ulshoeffer remained in America after the war, and in 1785 came to New York, where he resided, a teacher of music, until his death in 1836.

He married Margareth Miller, of Pennsylvania, who survived him many years and died in this city at the age of ninety-eight.

Their son, Michael Ulshoeffer, studied law in the office of T. W. Smith, at No. 3 Cedar Street, and afterwards became his partner.

In 1813 he was admitted as an attorney in the Mayor's Court or Court of Common Pleas, and in the same year in the Supreme Court of the State.*

He was appointed in 1814 a Notary Public, and in in 1815 a Master in Chancery, and served from 1815 to 1825 as Notary of the City Bank. In 1816 he was admitted as a counsellor-at-law in the Mayor's Court

---

* The various dates of admittance to practice in the different Courts have been inserted in the sketch of Judge Ulshoeffer as illustrative of the practice of another day and generation.

MICHAEL ULSHOEFFER.

and in the Supreme Court, and in 1817 to the United States Circuit and District Courts. In 1817 he was elected to the State Assembly, and was re-elected in 1818, 1819, 1820, and 1821.

Hammond, who was opposed politically to Judge Ulshoeffer, in his "History of Political Parties in the State of New York," several times refers to his career in the Legislature. He says that " The principal and most zealous of the members of the New York delegation (opponents of DeWitt Clinton) in 1818 were: Ogden Edwards, Peter Sharpe, and Michael Ulshoeffer," and again, that " In 1820, the most powerful and efficient men in opposition to endorsing the action of the Comptroller in auditing the accounts of Daniel D. Tompkins, late Governor, were Root, Sharpe, Romain, Ulshoeffer, J. T. Irving, and Seymour, and that for skill in argument, pungency of wit, and clear, sound, logical powers of mind, few men of that age would, he imagined, have excelled Oakley, Williams, Root, Spencer, Ulshoeffer, Romain, and McKown."

In General Wilson's " History of the City of New York," it is written that " When in 1820, a bill providing for a convention to revise the Constitution of the State was disapproved by the Council of Revision—Chancellor Kent writing the opinion with all the conservatism of a trained lawyer—the report of Michael Ulshoeffer, chairman of the select committee of the Assembly, combated the logic of the veto with great vigor, and the report was regarded as the abler State paper of the two."

In 1819, Mr. Ulshoeffer was admitted as solicitor and counsellor in chancery. Mr. Ulshoeffer was in partnership with William W. Boyd from 1823 until 1829, when

Mr. Boyd retired on account of ill-health. In 1821 he was appointed Corporation Attorney of the City of New York. In 1823, it was resolved by the Common Council that he should perform the duties of counsel to the Board during their pleasure. In 1825 he was formally appointed counsel to the Corporation, and the same year the offices of attorney and counsel to the Corporation were separated. He served until 1829.

In 1828 he was admitted an attorney and counsellor in the Superior Court of the City of New York. In 1834 he was appointed by the Governor, with the consent of the Senate, Associate Judge of the Court of Common Pleas and was re-appointed in 1843. In 1846 he was elected Judge of the Court of Common Pleas under the new Constitution and drew the shortest term, two years. He was chosen First Judge by his associates in 1838, and held the office continuously until the expiration of his service on the bench, December 31, 1849. His portrait was painted by Elliott at the request of members of the bar, and hangs in what was the Court room of the General Term of the Common Pleas.

As there were no regular reports of the Court of Common Pleas in his time, a few of his opinions appear in the first of E. D. Smith's Reports and in the Code Reporter and City Hall Reporter.

Judge Ulshoeffer never afterwards practiced law, but served on many boards and commissions and as a referee and arbitrator. He was one of the commissioners to appraise the lands taken for Central Park. He was one of the founders of the Law Institute of New York City. He joined the Tammany Society in 1817 and was elected Sachem in 1818.

The only public office he held after leaving the bench was as Commissioner of the Metropolitan Police in 1859 and 1860 under the Act of 1857. The Act of 1860 legislated the Board out of office.

He was a vestryman of St. Mark's Church for years, then warden. Afterwards a vestryman of Grace Church, until forced by age to retire. He served frequently as a delegate to the Diocesan Convention, where he was on the Committee for the Incorporation of Churches.

In politics he always claimed to be a Democrat, but insisted that often the party had deserted its principles. He voted for those he considered the best men without much regard to party. He was a War Democrat.

During his last years he spent much of his time in reading over and destroying his papers and correspondence, and left nothing concerning himself or others. Although he lent his books freely, he always refused to allow any of his private papers to go out of his hands, believing that much unnecessary trouble is caused by raking over men's lives, and that there is much to be forgiven and more to be forgotten.

He married Mary Ann Gracie in 1823 and had several children, some of whom survive.

He died in New York City, Sept. 6, 1881, at the age of eighty-eight years.

THE HONORABLE DANIEL P. INGRAHAM.

Daniel Phoenix Ingraham, third Judge of the Court of Common Pleas, was born in New York City April 22d, 1800. He was educated at a private school in Morristown, New Jersey, entered Columbia College at the age of thirteen, and was graduated in the class of 1817. During the next four years he studied law in the office of Hon. Richard Riker, Recorder of the City of New York. When of age, Mr. Ingraham was admitted to practice in the Court of Common Pleas, and later in the other Courts of the city.

He was elected Assistant Alderman from the Twelfth Ward in 1835, and the two following years represented the same ward in the Board of Aldermen. In 1838 Gov. Marcy appointed him Judge of the Court of Common Pleas in New York City to fill a vacancy. In 1843 he was re-appointed to hold office until 1846, when by the provisions of the new Constitution, the office became elective. The esteem in which he was generally held is shown by the fact that he was returned to the office by a large vote and re-elected in 1851. He was chosen First Judge of the Court two years later, and held the office until 1858, and was elected a Justice of the Supreme Court of the State in 1857 and re-elected in 1865. In 1870 Gov. Hoffman appointed him Presiding Justice of the Supreme Court of the First District in New York, a position which he filled with honor and

DANIEL P. INGRAHAM.

dignity until January 1, 1874, when, being over seventy years of age and not eligible to re-election, he retired to private life.

Judge Ingraham had many cases of the greatest importance tried before him; among others, that of Schuyler, who was accused by the New York & New Haven Railroad Company of issuing and selling $3,000,-000 worth of fraudulent stocks; of Cole for the murder of Hiscock; and of Stokes for the murder of Fiske. Judge Ingraham's decisions have been acknowledged to be among the soundest and most impartial in the judicial history of the State. His integrity was incorruptible, and, although he had many political opponents, he invariably compelled their respect and their acknowledgment of the honesty and purity of his public and private life, and his fidelity to the best interests of the community he served.

As a student, Judge Ingraham devoted much of his spare time to historical and geographical research, and was a member of the New York Historical Society and of the American Geographical Society. He was for many years one of the Elders of the Collegiate Dutch Church in the City of New York. On January 25, 1838, he married Miss Mary Hart Landon, of Connecticut, by whom he had three sons, all now living, and one of whom, Judge George L. Ingraham, was elected a Justice of the Superior Court in 1882, and of the Supreme Court in 1891, and is now one of the seven original members of the Appellate Division of the Supreme Court for the First Judicial District of New York.

Judge Daniel P. Ingraham died December 12, 1881. His portrait now hangs on the walls of the Supreme Court room, Appellate Division.

THE HONORABLE WILLIAM INGLIS.

William Inglis, fourth Judge of the Court of Common Pleas, was, it is believed, born in the city of New York. His father appears to have been John Inglis a native of Scotland, who was a merchant doing business in the lower part of the city as early as 1812, and for years thereafter; or this may have been the Judge's grandfather—for there was a John Inglis in New York in 1785, the only one of the name then living there. Judge Inglis was prepared for and entered Columbia College, being graduated with the class of 1821. His career as a student was distinguished, but he never fully realized the great expectations formed of his future, not so much from want of intellectual ability, as from a certain inertness that indisposed him to exertion where it could be dispensed with; and as he had a modest patrimony, and was careful and economical in his habits, he was able in that respect to do as he wished. His application in college, however, must have been close; and on his graduation he was a good classical scholar, and with other requirements had a knowledge of modern languages, speaking French fluently.

He was admitted to the bar in 1826, took an office in Pine Street, and during the thirteen years that followed until his appointment to the bench, held what might be called a highly respectable position at the bar, without being especially distinguished either as a lawyer or an advocate. When a heated political controversy arose about the policy of General Jackson towards the United States Bank, and the Whig party was formed, he took a somewhat prominent part in the formation and proceedings of that party; and it was probably due to that circumstance that he was selected as a proper person to fill the new judgeship in the Court of Common Pleas, then just created by an act of the Legislature, and to which he was appointed in 1839.

The appointment proved highly satisfactory, and he became a favorite Judge for the trial of causes. The leading and the more learned members of the bar especially liked to try causes before him, because they were sure that every point made by them, however learned or acute, would be fully comprehended and duly considered; and he was popular also with the jurors, for in his charge he made everything clear to them—in fact, he was what might be called a model Judge at *nisi prius*—intelligent, discriminating, patient, rarely interrupting and giving close attention to the evidence upon which the facts depended, and to the discussion of the questions of law that were raised, which it is for the Judge alone on the trial to decide. He was also very kind to young men, always willing to aid and to afford them every assistance, and invariably courteous.

He was not so satisfactory in other branches of his judicial duty. Except in settling a case or bill of exceptions for review, which could not be dispensed with, he did everything orally, as far as he could. Where cases were argued *in banc*, that is, before the three Judges together, to set aside a verdict or grant a new trial for some error of law at the trial, or errors of any kind that entitled the defeated party to a new trial, if he could have had his way, he would have rendered decision immediately upon the close of the argument, even when his colleagues thought that the points involved required a more deliberate examination, a careful perusal of the case as settled, looking into the authorities cited, and other things essential to a carefully matured judgment, which requires time and due deliberation. Judges *in banc* take the case, as it is said, and afterwards announce the result in a written opinion, showing upon what grounds they place their conclusion and judgment; but simply to endorse on the papers "reversed" or "affirmed," is not very satisfactory to the one who is defeated, nor even to the one who succeeds, as the case may be carried up to a higher Court. Yet this was all that he ever did, for it is said that he never gave a written opinion upon these final judgments and assigned as a reason for it that it was unnecessary, as no reports of the Court were then published, and it was merely writing an opinion to be filed among the papers. He overlooked the fact that a large part of the common law was made up in this way by the Judges having their conclusion, and the reasons for it, briefly stated in writing upon the record, long before any such thing as law reports were known, which began with the Year Books, and that it was from recorded memoranda of this kind, put in writing by order of the Judges, upon record, that Bracton, one of the earliest and the ablest of the early writers on the English law, was enabled to produce his celebrated trea-

WILLIAM INGLIS.

tise to show what the common law was. This omission on his part was the more marked because his associates never suffered a case that had been taken for further consideration to be decided without a written opinion by one of them, and sometimes two.

But notwithstanding this omission and the complaints made about it, he was a Judge that everybody liked. Mr. O'Conor then one of the great leaders of the bar, had a high opinion of his merit as a Judge, and so had all the lawyers, and particularly those who had the largest practice in the Court, and were the best able to judge.

He was always affable and ready to chat with any member of the profession as the opportunity offered; and in this easy familiarity made little or no distinction between the highest and the humblest member of the bar. He was fond of what is called gossip, and had a large amount of local information respecting prominent New York families, could tell with whom they had intermarried, and had a remarkable memory for the smallest details which would scarcely be expected from a bachelor who rarely went into society or was seen at any social gathering or party. He seemed to take pleasure in this kind of information and retained in his memory many details which would escape from the minds of others.

As his term was about to expire (the appointment was then for but five years), there was a very general desire on the part of the bar for his reappointment, but the Democratic party having been then for some years out of power, there was a determination to make full use of the newly acquired patronage for political purposes and to make no distinction even in respect to the bench. Two lawyers who were active politicians, became candidates: Thomas W. Waterman, author of a work on "Injunctions," long since superseded, and Thomas Jefferson Smith, afterwards a Judge of the Marine Court; both of them inferior to Judge Inglis in legal knowledge and ability. As it was a local appointment, the jurisdiction of the Court being confined to the city of New York, it was the custom of the Governor to appoint the person agreed upon by the representatives of the city of New York, of his own party, in the Legislature. It so happened however, that Waterman and Smith who were very influential politicians, divided the New York delegation so that they were equally balanced both in the Senate and Assembly, and as neither party would give way to the other, no agreement could be arrived at. In this state of things, it was hoped that Judge Inglis might be reappointed, especially as the Democratic lawyers of New York had strongly urged his reappointment. But Governor Bouck was unwilling to make any exception and would appoint no one who was not a Democrat. He sought the advice of Governor Marcy, a very distinguished man of large political experience, afterwards Secretary of State under President Polk, and he recommended the appointment of Charles P. Daly, a young man then twenty-seven years of age, to the delegation for the appointment. Judge Daly had been a member of the Legislature the previous year, and as many of the delegation had been members with him, they accepted this compromise and agreed upon him. Judge Daly declined the appointment when offered,

74

being a friend of Judge Inglis whose appointment he had warmly advocated, but afterwards accepted it at that Judge's personal request, Judge Inglis being satisfied that his own reappointment could not be obtained.

On leaving the bench Judge Inglis took an office in John Street, which he kept thereafter for many years, doing, however, comparatively little or no business except an occasional reference, but passed a large part of his time in the Society Library, in which he became a trustee in 1837, and continued until 1855, and held for many years the office of Secretary of the Board of Trustees, the distinguished New York scholar Gulian C. Ver Planck being its chairman. The Society Library having no president, the chairman of the board was its highest officer.

Judge Inglis was an omnivorous reader and preferred being among his books than anywhere else. He was rarely thereafter seen about the Courts, seldom if ever went into society or mingled much with men. He had an intimate young friend, a lawyer, and when taking exercise in the Park upon the Battery, his favorite resort, they were almost invariably together. It might be supposed that so accomplished a man with such a widely extended and varied amount of information would have devoted his time at least in part, to some literary work or to the production of a law book that was wanted and could be useful; but he appears to have had no inclination for anything of the kind.

While he was on the bench he was invited by Columbia College to deliver a literary address upon some particular occasion which he accepted, and a friend of his who heard it said regretfully that it was a

75

failure; that it manifested learning enough but wanted constructiveness, and that the general impression of those present seemed to be that of disappointment. It may be therefore said that with all his requirements he lacked naturally the art, or had never taken the trouble to acquire it, of making use of his knowledge in producing something even for his own gratification, or which might be useful or prove agreeable or entertaining to others. His life would probably have been a pleasanter and happier one if he had; for after he left the bench, and especially as he advanced in years, he became moody, and it is said in his latter years, to have been under the infatuation that he would eventually come to want, a condition not to be apprehended in a man of his prudence and economical habits. A few years before his death he went to New Jersey and took up his residence at Hoboken, and is said to have died in 1863.

Charles P. Daly L.L.D.

THE HONORABLE CHARLES P. DALY, LL.D.

Charles P. Daly, fifth Judge of the Court of Common Pleas, was born in the City of New York, Oct. 31st, 1816. His parents had emigrated from the North of Ireland in 1814 and settled in this city, where the father was a master carpenter. His ancestors were the O'Dalys of County Galway, a family notable in Irish history for its many scholars, bards and legislators.

He began his education at a private school, where he had for classmates among others the late Cardinal John McCloskey and the late James T. Brady.

The death of his father, however, interrupted his studies; and, high-minded even as a boy, he was unwilling to depend upon a widowed stepmother. He went to Savannah, Georgia, where he obtained employment as a clerk, but chafing under ill-treatment, he shipped as a sailor before the mast and for the next three years followed the sea. His naturally active mind was, in the meantime, busy collecting knowledge and his original observations on the geographical and historical features of the many places visited in the course of his voyages, laid the foundation for the interest in those subjects in after life.

On his return to New York he apprenticed himself to learn the trade—which was before the days of steel pens and envelopes—of preparing quills for writing and making sealing wax and wafers, and in his leisure hours

77

continued his studies. He joined a literary society, and soon developed remarkable aptitude of mind and great readiness as a debater. His exceptional abilities attracted the attention of William Soulé, a member of the bar, who earnestly urged him to study law, even offering to defray the cost of his going through a collegiate course preparatory to beginning his legal studies. He was, however, too proud to put himself under such an obligation, but upon the expiration of his term of indenture became a clerk in Mr. Soulé's office and devoted himself with characteristic assiduity to his professional studies.

The student of law was at that time required to devote seven years to his preparation for the bar, but so rapid was Mr. Daly's progress that upon the motion of Mr. Rowley, senior member of the firm, the rule was relaxed in his case by Chief Justice Nelson, and he was admitted to the bar at the end of three and one-half years of study. He at once formed a partnership with Thomas McElrath, afterward the founder, with Horace Greeley, of the New York "Tribune." He rapidly attained prominence at the bar, and became noted for the lucidity and compactness of his legal documents and his ability in the trial of causes. His notable eloquence seems also to have been a natural qualification, which at once brought him prominence and renown.

He was elected to the Legislature in 1843, and after serving his term there was offered a nomination for Congress, in a district where his election was certain, which he declined. In 1844 expired the term of Judge Inglis, of the Court of Common Pleas, and, although strongly urged to re-appoint him, Gov. Bouck offered the vacant seat to Mr. Daly, then but twenty-eight years of age. He at first declined the honor on the ground of his youth and inexperience, at the same time strongly urging the prior claims of Inglis. But upon being urged by the Governor, who would not re-appoint Judge Inglis, and by Judge Inglis himself who preferred Mr. Daly to any other possible successor, he accepted the honorable office which he continued to hold for forty-one years.

When by the Constitution of 1846 the office was made elective, Judge Daly was promptly chosen by popular vote for a term of six years; and was three times thereafter re-elected for similar terms. In 1871 the public appreciation of his ability, fidelity and integrity was shown in an unprecedented fashion. His last appearance before the popular vote was well befitting his career. After the exposure of Tweed and his satellites Judge Daly was nominated to succeed himself by all factions in the Democracy and by the Republicans. Every vote cast in the City of New York in the election of 1871 bore the name of the Chief Justice of the Common Pleas.

Judge Daly became "First Judge" of the Court of Common Pleas upon the resignation of Judge Daniel Ingraham in 1857, and was re-chosen to the post in 1871, with title of "Chief Justice." He would undoubtedly have long continued in office had not the State Constitution of 1867 prescribed the resignation of a Judge when seventy years of age. His judicial career exceeded by ten years that of Judge Story of Massachusetts, and by an equal term that of Lord Mansfield in England. Few jurists have had the good fortune to

79

be so honored as Judge Charles P. Daly. "The illustrious career of Judge Samuel Nelson reached to within a few months of a full half century of service, but embraced his term in the Supreme Court of the United States as well as that in the Supreme Court of the State of New York." These words are quoted from an address made by Mr. William Allen Butler, at a meeting of the bar held in the Court on Dec. 30th, 1885, the last day of Judge Daly's official life. The call to this meeting was signed not only by Mr. Butler, but by David Dudley Field, Clarence A. Seward, F. R. Coudert, James C. Carter, Joseph H. Choate, Elihu Root, John L. Cadwallader, John W. Sterling, Charles C. Beaman, and many others of equal prominence. Ex-President Chester A. Arthur presided. The meeting was thronged. Addresses were made by Mr. Butler, Mr. Field, the late Judge O'Gorman, and others. An extended account of this meeting appears elsewhere in this volume.

In the evening a banquet was given at Delmonico's to the retiring Chief Justice. It was unparalleled in the sense that it was given by the Judges of the Supreme and Superior Courts, the Court of Common Pleas, the Court of General Sessions and the Recorder and the Surrogate. The guests, with two exceptions, were all Judges. Twenty-eight sat at the table. The exceptions were the clerks of the Common Pleas and of the Superior Courts, Messrs. Nathaniel Jarvis, Jr., and Thomas Boese.

Judge Daly has been noted for the suavity of his manner, the lucidity of his style, the integrity of his life, his activity, industry and thorough knowledge of the law.

He has written much, has been connected with many organizations, varying in their range from the Friendly Sons of St. Patrick to the American Geographical Society, over both of which bodies he has presided as president, and is to-day a member of the Union, the Century, and other clubs, and is as active as many of those who are much his junior in years.

The degree of LL. D. was conferred on him by Columbia College in 1860.

His published works are: The Ancient Feudal and the Modern Banking System Compared; The Judicial Tribunals of New York from 1693 to 1848; The Settlement of the Jews in North America; History of the Surrogate's Court of New York; Naturalization, its past History and its Present State; Biographical Sketch of Gulian C. Verplanck; Barratry, Its Origin, History and Meaning in the Maritime Law; Origin of Corporations for the Promotion of the Useful Arts; The Jews of New York; Sketch of Henry Peters Gray, the Artist; When was the Drama Introduced in America; Early History of Cartography or What we Know of Maps and Map-making before the time of Mercator; Biographical Sketch of Charles O'Conor; Are the Southern Privateersmen Pirates; History of Physical Geography; Have we a Portrait of Columbus; Is the Monroe Doctrine Involved in the Controversy Between Venezuela and Great Britain; Wants of a Botanical Garden in New York, and many speeches and lectures with cases argued and determined in the New York Court of Common Pleas, in 16 Vols., the labor of which under his supervision has been mainly performed by Ephraim A. Jacob, now a Justice of the Court of Special Sessions of the City of New York.   A portrait of Judge Daly, painted by Daniel Huntington, hangs in what was the Court room of the General Term of the Court of Common Pleas.

THE HONORABLE LEWIS B. WOODRUFF, LL.D.

Lewis B. Woodruff, sixth Judge of the Court of Common Pleas, was born in Litchfield, Conn., June 19th, 1809. He was educated in the Morris Academy at Litchfield, and entered Yale College, where he was graduated with high honors in the class of 1830. During his course he displayed great proficiency in mathematics, which was in after life his favorite pastime. At the famous Law School in Litchfield, under the instruction of Judge Gould, he laid the foundation of the scholarly learning which so distinguished his judicial career, and on completing his studies in 1832 he was admitted to the Bar of Connecticut. He soon after came to New York City, and formed a partnership with Hon. Willis Hall, which continued until 1836. He afterwards became associated with Mr. George Wood, then at the head of the bar, and Mr. Richard Goodman, under the style of " Woodruff & Goodman."

In 1849 he was elected Judge of the Court of Common Pleas, to succeed Hon. Michael Ulshoeffer, and held that office for six years, 1850–1855. Among his associates were Daniel P. Ingraham, Charles P. Daly and John R. Brady, and during his term he gave notable construction to the Code and Mechanic's Lien law, then both new.

At the close of his term of office in the Court of Common Pleas he was elected Judge of the Superior Court, where he had for associates Judges Oakley, Duer, Bosworth, Hoffman, Slosson and Pierrepont. This office he also filled for six years, 1856–1861.

At the close of this judicial term he resumed the practice of his profession, and the reputation he had at that time acquired attracted to him a large and profitable business. As counsel in the trial of causes, he was engaged in some of the most important cases of the day. He remained at the bar, associated as counsel with Hon. Charles F. Sanford, and his son, Charles H. Woodruff, practicing under the firm name of "Sanford & Woodruff," for six years, 1862–1867.

In January, 1868, he was appointed a Judge of the Court of Appeals to fill a vacancy occasioned by the resignation of Hon. John K. Porter, and held the office until the close of the following year.

In December, 1869, he was nominated by President Grant and confirmed by the Senate, to the office, then newly created, of Judge of the Circuit Court of the United States for the Second Judicial Circuit, embracing the States of New York, Connecticut and Vermont. This appointment, urged with singular unanimity, spontaneity and earnestness by the bar and leading men of the day, was greeted with high encomiums by the press. This office he held until his death, September 10th, 1875.

His great learning, remarkable power of analysis, deep discernment and excellent judgment made him invaluable as a counsellor, while these qualities of his mind, reinforced by habits of study and industry and sterling integrity, insured his high reputation on the bench during his whole judicial career. So close was his application that he never allowed himself needed rest, his study being habitually prolonged until late into the night. "He went to the very bottom of every subject with which he undertook to deal. He cared not for a multiplicity of details; they never clogged his perception of a general bearing, and never one of them was deprived of the exact degree of weight to which it was relatively entitled. Law was to him what music or art is to some natures; it engrossed him, and was a province in which he moved a king and a master." In the expression of his legal conclusions he was clear and precise, and his written opinions are models of demonstration.

To his mathematical genius were added mechanical skill and ingenuity of such high order, that it was said of him that "a good mechanic was lost when he studied law." This talent was developed at an early age, and his boyhood home contained many labor-saving devices, evidences of his inventive skill. In after life this fitted him to deal with the cases of admiralty and particularly of patent law, which formed so large a part of his duties as Circuit Judge.

Dignified in his bearing, and exacting the respect which was his due, he was in the family circle tender and affectionate, everywhere generous, kind and helpful. An appearance of austerity on the bench but masked the kindness and gentleness of his heart. Himself laborious, painstaking and exhaustive, he had little patience with indifference and negligence in the performance of duty in others.

Devoted to his home and home joys, genial and cordial, he was the delight of the social circle, and his loving welcome, hospitable board and ever open door kept warm hearts constantly about him.

In the summer of 1875, broken in health, his vigorous mind and untiring energy having overtaxed a strong body, he went to his summer home in Litchfield, and there slowly but surely failed in strength, until on the 10th day of September he passed away, esteemed, revered and beloved, as few men are, by all who knew him.

His honors were chiefly professional and judicial, though in 1860 he received the honorary degree of Doctor of Laws from Columbia College.

He began political life as a National Republican, continued with that party under the name of Free Soil Whig, and on the formation of the present Republican party became and always continued its firm friend and supporter.

Educated a Congregationalist, he first became a member of its communion. On removal to New York, he became connected with the Presbyterian Church, and later transferred his church membership to the Collegiate Reformed Protestant Dutch Church, of which he was an elder and one of the most valued and trusted advisors of its councils.

JOHN R. BRADY.

THE HONORABLE JOHN R. BRADY.

Thomas S. Brady, born in Ireland, was admitted to the New York Bar in 1826, was a Justice of the Peace, became an Alderman for the City of New York when the office meant something more than it does to-day, was a remarkable linguist, was at one period a teacher, teaching among others the late Cardinal McCloskey, and died in the city of his adoption. His three sons became lawyers and were all remarkable men. The eldest, Thomas Brady, before he attained distinction at the bar, was appointed into the United States Marine Corps and lived and died an officer of the navy.

The second son, James T. Brady, one of the most brilliant of all the members of the New York Bar, became Corporation Counsel of the City of New York, and in 1860 was the candidate for Governor of the State on the Hard-shell or Pro-slavery Democratic ticket. It is said of Mr. James T. Brady that he never lost a cause in which he was before a jury for more than a week—for in that time everything was seen through his eyes.

John Riker Brady, seventh Judge of the Court of Common Pleas, was born in the City of New York in 1821, was admitted to the bar in 1842, and immediately went into partnership with Mr. Maurice and with his brother, James T. Brady, the firm being Brady, Maurice & Brady. Mr. Maurice afterwards withdrew, and the two brothers continued in business alone, until the younger one was called to the bench. Elected in 1855 to the Court of Common Pleas, Judge John R. Brady was re-elected in 1869, and before his second term had expired he was elected to the Supreme Bench. At his second election to the Common Pleas Bench, he received the endorsement of the Republicans and of all factions of the Democratic party, was unopposed, and consequently elected by an immense vote. At the expiration of his first term on the Supreme Court Bench in 1877, he again received the unanimous nomination of all parties, and had he lived but a few months longer would have retired, having reached the constitutional age of seventy. His career on the bench covered a period of over thirty-five years. In 1863, he married Katherine Lydig, daughter of Philip M. Lydig, and sister of the wife of Judge Charles P. Daly, who sat on the bench of the Common Pleas for over forty years.

Judge Brady was one of the best trial Judges known in the history of the New York Bar; many of his opinions attracted widespread attention, and were founded on common sense and natural justice rather than on fine technical points, though he never allowed anything to interfere with his sense of duty.

Judge Brady was a member of many social organizations, was one of the founders of the Manhattan Club, one of the presidents of the Lambs' Club, and served several terms as president of the Friendly Sons of St. Patrick.

He died after an illness of less than twenty-four hours, being afflicted with an abscess on the brain, in the Hanover apartment house, in the City of New York, on March 16th (1891).

A portrait of Judge Brady for a period adorned the Court room of the General Term of the Common Pleas, but on the abolition of the Court was removed to the rooms of the Appellate Division of the Supreme Court.

THE HONORABLE HENRY HILTON.

Henry Hilton, eighth Judge of the Court of Common Pleas, was born in October, 1824, at Newburgh, in Orange County, N. Y. His father was Scotch-Irish; his mother, Janet Graham, a woman of singular intelligence and force of character, was Scotch. When Henry was a small child his father removed to New York, and was engaged in business here until his death. living in Wooster Street.

Henry Hilton was the youngest of four sons, all of whom were bred to professional life. The eldest son, James, was for many years a Judge in Iowa, and is still living, at an advanced age, at Hilton, Monroe County, Iowa. The second son, Joseph Hilton, became a physician, and was at one time coroner of New York. The third son, Archibald, became prominent as a lawyer in this city early in life, and some of the older lawyers at the bar still speak of him as the best practitioner they ever knew. He died when a comparatively young man.

Henry Hilton was admitted to the bar in 1846, and for some years acted as Master in Chancery. He soon acquired an extensive and lucrative practice, being engaged in many important litigations, notably that in which it was sought to condemn the property known as "Jones' Wood" for the purposes of a public park. He

HENRY HILTON.

successfully resisted the attempt on behalf of the property-owners.

In the early fifties he married Miss Ellen Banker, a daughter of Edward Banker, of Banker & Schermerhorn, and a sister of James H. Banker, who afterwards became prominent as a financier and capitalist, being president of the Bank of New York, and a director in the New York Central Railroad Company and in many other financial institutions.

He was elected a Judge of the Common Pleas in 1857 by a majority of about 17,000 over William M. Allen. He edited the two volumes of "Hilton's Reports," covering the period from 1855 to 1860, and the head-notes in those volumes are still regarded as models of concise and accurate statement. At the end of his term, he resumed the practice of the law, taking into partnership Douglas Campbell, the son of Judge William W. Campbell who in the Judge's youth had been his senior partner, and Joseph Bell, who had been Assistant United States District Attorney for the Southern District of New York, and was later appointed by President Arthur Judge of the Supreme Court for New Mexico, where he died. Douglas Campbell will be best known to posterity as the author of " The Puritan in Holland, England and America," a work wholly written while he was struggling against the fatal illness to which he finally succumbed.

Judge Hilton is, perhaps, most widely known from his relations to Alexander T. Stewart. Mrs. Hilton was the cousin of Mrs. Stewart, and through that relationship the Judge was early brought into social intimacy with Mr. Stewart, and became his legal adviser before he was elected a Judge of the Court of Common Pleas. After his retirement from the bench, in addition to his office in the firm of Hilton, Campbell & Bell, he also had an office in the mercantile house of Mr. Stewart, and continued in most intimate professional and personal relations until his death. Mr. Stewart, who died in April, 1876, left him a large legacy in his Will, and Mrs. Stewart, shortly after her husband's death, at the request of her husband, as she stated, transferred to Judge Hilton all interest in the mercantile business. Thereupon Judge Hilton wholly abandoned his profession and devoted himself to mercantile pursuits. He is one of the very few who, after being trained to and passing many years in a profession, have been successful men of business. He continued in mercantile business until about 1883 when he was succeeded by his sons, and his son-in-law, who have since continued the business under the firm names of—Sylvester, Hilton & Co., and Hilton, Hughes & Co. His son, Col. Albert B. Hilton, is now the head of the firm.

Judge Hilton has a splendid country seat at Saratoga, known as Woodlawn Park. It consists of about a thousand acres, and has something like fifteen miles of wooded drives which are thrown open to the public, greatly adding to the attractions of that famous resort.

Judge Hilton was always noted for his self-reliance, mental and physical energy, and great rapidity of thought and action. While somewhat active in politics he has never been an aspirant for political honors nor a seeker for popularity. He belongs to the Century, the Press and New York Clubs; and his religious affiliations are with the Protestant Episcopal Church.

He has three sons living, Ed ward B., Henry G., and Albert B. Hilton; and two daughters, Cornelia, the wife of John M. Hughes, and Josephine H., the wife of Judge Horace Russell.

THE HONORABLE ALBERT CARDOZO, LL.D.

Albert Cardozo, LL.D., ninth Judge of the Court of Common Pleas, was born in Philadelphia, December 21st, 1828.

While yet a child he was brought to the City of New York. His parents being poor, he was obliged to leave school at an early age, and to depend on his own exertions. Determining upon the law as a profession, he was admitted to the bar soon after attaining his majority in 1849. He was successful in his practice, and in the Autumn of 1863, when less than thirty-five years of age, was elected to the Bench of the Common Pleas. He resigned from the Court of Common Pleas in 1867, to take the nomination for the Supreme Court, to which he was elected, and took his seat on the first of January, 1868.

When a Judge of the Supreme Court, Judge Cardozo was accused of complicity with the Tweed ring, but the widely agitated investigation was dropped upon his resignation. Instead of leaving New York, as it was generally understood that he would do, he presently became active again, both at the bar and in politics.

In 1874 he formed a partnership with Richard S. Newcomb, and in 1878 was made a member of the General Committee of Tammany Hall, and shortly afterward was elected Sachem of Tammany Society.

Judge Cardozo died in the City of New York on November 8th, 1885.

HOOPER C. VAN VORST, LL.D.

THE HONORABLE HOOPER C. VAN VORST, LL.D.

Hooper C. Van Vorst, LL.D., tenth Judge of the Court of Common Pleas was born in Schenectady, in the State of New York, on December 3d, 1817.

He was graduated at Union College in 1839, and immediately after graduation began the study of law in his native town. In 1841 he removed to Albany, was admitted to the bar and shortly afterwards appointed by the municipal board attorney and counsel to the city, which office he held for several years. Coming to the City of New York in 1853, he soon acquired a large practice. In 1868 he was appointed by Gov. Fenton Justice of the Court of Common Pleas and served on that bench for one year. In 1871 he was elected for a full term of fourteen years to the Bench of the Superior Court of the City of New York.

During a large part of his connection with the latter Court, however, acting under the appointment of the Governor of the State, Judge Van Vorst sat in the Supreme Court.

A strict Presbyterian, Judge Van Vorst, soon after he came to New York, united with the Fifth Avenue Presbyterian Church, then under the pastorate of Dr. James W. Alexander, but now for many years under the charge of Rev. Dr. John Hall.

Besides being identified with the local church, he was

a Commissioner for the Presbytery of New York to the General Assembly in May, 1883, at Saratoga, and was for many years a member of the Board of Foreign Missions and a Trustee of the Children's Aid Society of the Presbyterian Church. He was also one of the founders of the Holland Society and was its president for several years.

Judge Van Vorst was noted for his sincerity, for his simplicity of manners, for his warm and constant friendships, and for his active sympathy with charitable and religious concerns. His judicial course was characterized by learning, impartiality and inflexible adherence to the law.

The degree of LL.D., was conferred upon Judge Van Vorst by Union College.

He was twice married and left surviving him a widow and several children. His son Frederick B. Van Vorst is now engaged in the practice of law in New York City.

Judge Van Vorst died in New York City on October 26th, 1889.

GEORGE C. BARRETT.

THE HONORABLE GEORGE C. BARRETT.

Though yet in the prime of life, considerably under sixty years of age, Judge Barrett has already passed nearly thirty years of his active life upon the bench. Elected Civil Justice at the age of twenty-five, identified for nearly two years with the Court of Common Pleas, he is now (1896) serving the eleventh year of his second term as Justice of the Supreme Court.

George Carter Barrett, eleventh Judge of the Court of Common Pleas, was born in Ireland, July 28, 1838. His father was the Rev. Gilbert Carter Barrett, a clergyman of the Church of England who, soon after the birth of his son became a missionary to the Indian tribes of Canada. His grandfather, Lieut. John Carter Barrett, was an officer in the English army during the Napoleonic wars and was awarded a medal for bravery on the field of Waterloo.

Judge Barrett began his education in London, West Canada, afterwards attending the Columbia Grammar School in New York City from whence he entered Columbia College. He left college at the end of freshman year and began the study of law. At this period he in large part supported himself by engaging in various literary ventures, writing serials, short stories, and novels and contributing to newspapers articles on topics of current interest.

After his admission to the bar he practiced for several years with success, but in 1863 was elected Justice of the Sixth Judicial District and from that year, excepting for a short intermission, 1871–72, has been continuously identified with our judiciary.

During this period, 1871–72, Judge Barrett became strongly identified with state and national politics. He was president of the Young Men's Municipal Reform Association in its memorable contest against the Tweed ring. He was a member of the Committee of Seventy of that time, and in association with Messrs. A. R. Lawrence, Francis C. Barlow, and Wheeler H. Peckham, acted as its counsel. He was also counsel for John Foley in his celebrated injunction suit against the ring.

Judge Barrett was married on November 30, 1865, to Miss Gertrude Fairfield, a daughter of Sumner Lincoln Fairfield, the poet and literateur.

Elected Judge of the Court of Common Pleas in 1869, after a service of nearly two years, more accurately, one year and nine months, he resigned with the intention of resuming the active practice of the profession. In 1871, however, he was elected Judge of the Supreme Court for the term of fourteen years, and was again in 1885, re-elected for another full term of fourteen years.

Identified for nearly a quarter of a century with the Supreme Court, although at all times possessed of unusual political power yet unsullied in reputation either as man, lawyer, or judge, it is not an unfitting tribute that Judge Barrett should be one of the original seven members of the Appellate Division of the Supreme Court of the First Judicial District of the State of New York.

FREDERICK W. LOEW.

THE HONORABLE FREDERICK W. LOEW.

Frederick William Loew, twelfth Judge of the Court of Common Pleas, was born in Alsace, December 20, 1834, and when about three years of age was brought by his parents to the United States.

His ancestry on both sides sprang from old Alsatian stock residing in Strasburg in Alsace. Many of them occupied high social and political positions in their ancestral city and other parts of France.

When about sixteen years old he lost his father, Frederick J. Loew, and was left with his mother and four younger brothers. He was educated in English, French, and German schools of New York City.

Having artistic tastes of a high order he determined to adopt engraving as a profession, and accordingly studied under one of the most talented engravers in the city. He applied himself so industriously to his art and attained such proficiency, that before he was twenty years old he received two silver medals and a handsome edition of Webster's dictionary for works of his exhibited at the American Institute and other expositions. The dies for medallions, etc., exhibited at the American Institute, was announced as having been cut and exposed by him expressly for the competition and he carried off the highest prize for the same as against the works of some of the most celebrated engravers of the country.

His close application however, and the habit of constantly stooping over his artistic work, had seriously impaired his health, and by advice of his physician he undertook a journey South.

Being a passenger on board the ill-fated steamer "Crescent City," he was shipwrecked on the Bahama banks on December 7, 1855, and after two nights and days of privation was finally taken from the wreck by a wrecking schooner to the island of Nassau. He sailed from thence to Havana, and later to New Orleans, where for some time he was seriously ill. The excitement and hardship, however, had called out all the latent energy of his system, and thus what was at first supposed would prove fatal tended to his recovery.

Returning home, he was obliged to choose a more active profession than art and entered upon the law. After holding a position as a law clerk in the sheriff's office for a time, devoting his leisure to professional study, he was admitted to the bar in 1860. From the start his practice was attended with success; his specialty was the examination of titles to real estate and conveyancing.

In the fall of 1863, he was elected by a large majority for a term of six years, Justice of the Fifth Judicial District Court of New York City, comprising the Seventh, Eleventh, and Thirteenth Wards. Under his able and faithful management the business of the Court increased steadily from year to year, as is shown by the official records.

In the spring of 1867 he was chosen by the electors of the Twelfth Assembly District as a member of the Constitutional Convention of 1867–68, in the work of which body he took an active part. In November, 1869, he was appointed by Governor Hoffman Judge of the Court of Common Pleas, to fill the unexpired term of Hon. George C. Barrett, resigned, and at the general election in the same month was chosen by a large popular vote for a full term of six years, commencing January 1, 1870.

As Justice of the Court of Common Pleas, Judge Loew made good his highly creditable record in former offices, and tried many notable and difficult cases with marked ability and impartiality. His decisions were very seldom reversed by the Court of Appeals. In October, 1875, he was appointed by Governor Tilden to hold a special term for the trial of jury causes in the Supreme Court.

In 1875, he was renominated by the Democracy for Justice of the Court of Common Pleas for the term of fourteen years, but owing to the sweeping victory of the combination of Republicans and Independent Democrats which had been made, he was unsuccessful, although he led the entire ticket by several thousand votes, and he therefore returned to active practice at the bar.

In 1877, after repeated refusals, he was finally persuaded to accept the Democratic nomination for Register of New York City and County, and notwithstanding a similar combination to that of 1875 had been entered into between the Republicans and Independent Democrats, he was, after a very excited and closely contested canvass, elected by several thousand majority, serving through the years 1878–79–80.

Some time after the expiration of his term of office

his health, never robust, at last gave way and he was obliged to discontinue active practice and seek relief in travel. He has since resided mostly in Paris, making occasional visits to New York or traveling throughout Europe and the Orient.

Judge Loew was careful and conscientious. His motto, " Whatever is worth doing at all is worth doing well," found ample expression in his judicial life. The unqualified, painstaking, and intense devotion to details which won him distinction in his first calling, characterized the whole of his public life.

He was married in New York City, December 19, 1867, to Julia Augusta, daughter of the late Jacob Vanderpoel, formerly Dock Commissioner, and a descendant of an old Holland Dutch family which settled in New Amsterdam in the earliest days of the colony.

THE HONORABLE CHARLES H. VAN BRUNT.

Charles H. Van Brunt, thirteenth Judge of the Court of Common Pleas, was born in 1836, at Bay Ridge, now a part of Brooklyn, in a house erected by one of his ancestors and which was until recently in Judge Van Brunt's possession.

Prepared for college in Brooklyn he was graduated at the University of the City of New York in the class of 1856. After studying law with the firm of Leonard & Hoffman, the head of which was formerly Commissioner of Appeals and a Judge of the Supreme Court; the other partner being Hon. John T. Hoffman, afterwards Governor of New York, he was admitted to the bar in 1860.

Judge Van Brunt continued in the office of Leonard & Hoffman for some years as confidential clerk and eventually became a partner in the firm, remaining in the practice of his profession until 1869, when he was appointed Judge of the Common Pleas to fill a vacancy caused by the election of Judge Brady to the Supreme Court. While at the bar he had an active practice, serving at one time as counsel to the City Chamberlain. Judge Van Brunt, in 1870, was elected for the full term of fourteen years and served on the bench of the Common Pleas until 1883, when he was elected to the Supreme Court. Judge Van Brunt, despite the discrepancy in their years, was an intimate friend of the elder Judge Ingraham, and has served on the bench with both of the Judges Ingraham—father and son.

He has been twice married, has several children, and is now one of the original seven members of the Appellate Division of the Supreme Court for the First Judicial District of New York. He is also one of the council of the University of the City of New York. He is a member of the Manhattan and Lotus Clubs, New York Yacht Club, and of the St. Nicholas Society. His only son, Arthur H. Van Brunt, is a practicing lawyer. Judge Van Brunt has been conspicuous for promptitude, energy, industry, and extraordinary facility in dispatching business with rapidity.

JOSEPH F. DALY, LL.D.

THE HONORABLE JOSEPH F. DALY, LL.D.

Joseph F. Daly, fourteenth Judge and last Chief Justice of the Court of Common Pleas, was born December 3, 1840, at Plymouth, North Carolina. His father was Captain Denis Daly, of Limerick, Ireland, who having been in early life appointed purser's clerk in the British navy, resigned to engage in the merchant service, built and sailed his own vessels, and finally settled in Plymouth as wharfinger, shipowner and merchant, and died in 1841. His maternal grandfather was Lieut. John Duffey of the 101st Regiment, stationed in Montego Bay, Jamaica, W. I., where the Judge's mother was born. The family removed to New York in 1849, and he commenced as law clerk with S. W. & R. B. Roosevelt in 1855, and studied law with them until 1862, when he was admitted to the bar. On the retirement of the firm from business in 1865 he succeeded to their practice. In 1867, he formed a co-partnership with George F. Noyes, and after the latter's death established the well-known firm of Daly, Henry & Olin. He was counsel for the Citizen's Association, an organization for municipal reform, from 1864 to 1870, and was attorney for the Chemical Bank and other prominent clients.

He became prominent as a legal adviser and an advocate of important measures of municipal reform. Among his prominent cases were the prosecutions of public officials before the Governor in 1865 (reported in 19 Abbott's Practice Reps., 376); injunctions against waste by municipal officers, he having instituted the first action of the kind, with John Hecker as plaintiff, in 1865 (18 Abbott's Practice Reps., 369). His private practice included important questions, among them the constitutionality of legislative appropriation of private wharf property for the canal district without compensation to owners (Roosevelt *v.* Goddard, 52 Barbour's Reps., 534). His practice from 1862 to 1870 covered all branches of the law. The State Constitution of 1869 increased the number of Judges of the Court of Common Pleas from three to six, and one of the nominations of the Democratic party was tendered to and accepted by Mr. Daly. His associates on the ticket were Hamilton W. Robinson and Richard L. Larremore, who were all elected on May 17, 1870, together with Charles H. Van Brunt, who was chosen to fill a vacancy.

Thus, at the age of twenty-nine he began a judicial career, which at the present writing (1896) has exceeded a quarter of a century. At the expiration of his term in 1884, Judge Daly was again elected and by a highly complimentary vote, inasmuch as he and Judge Larremore, his associate on the bench, were the only successful candidates on the ticket on which they ran. In 1890, he was chosen by his associates Chief Judge of the Court. Judge Daly is a man of force, industry, integrity, and learning, noted for his love of literature, and his interest in the drama, with which his brother, Augustin Daly, is connected; for his exquisite tastes, and especially for his collection of rare prints, books and pictures. As a Judge he is noted for his amiable temper—and has ever preserved an unvarying dignity of demeanor, always mingled with great courtesy and consideration, especially toward the younger members of the bar. He is a lucid reasoner, and one of the most thoroughly equipped lawyers on the New York bench.

Judge Daly's idea of the duties of both bench and bar was laconically expressed by himself on the closing of the Court over which he presided in what must hereafter be accepted as a legal aphorism—" A courageous bar makes an incorruptible judiciary."

It is very remarkable that while Judge Charles P. Daly sat on the Common Pleas Bench for over forty years, Judge Joseph F. Daly has held the next longest term of the twenty-three Judges identified with the later history of the Court. He received the degree of LL.D. from St. John's College at Fordham in 1883; was one of the founders and incorporators of the Players' Club, with Edwin Booth and others; is the President of the Catholic Club; a member of the Geographical Society, the Southern Club, the Friendly Sons of St. Patrick; a member of the New York Law Institute; honorary member of the Association of the Bar of the City of New York; manager of the Roman Catholic Orphan Asylum; member of the Advisory Board of St. Vincent's Hospital; member of the Democratic Club, and other social and literary organizations. By the Constitution of 1894, Judge Daly was transferred to the Supreme Court, and, together with Judge McAdam, late of the Superior Court, and Judge Bischoff, of the

Common Pleas, forms the Appellate Term, which reviews the decisions of the lower Courts.

Judge Daly has been twice married: first in 1873 to Miss Emma Robinson Barker, a stepdaughter of Judge Hamilton W. Robinson. She died in 1886, leaving three children. Second, in 1890, to Miss Mary Louise Smith, daughter of Edgar M. Smith, of New York.

HAMILTON W. ROBINSON.

THE HONORABLE HAMILTON W. ROBINSON.

Hamilton W. Robinson, fifteenth Judge of the Court of Common Pleas, was born in Albany, N. Y., November 25, 1814, son of James W. Robinson, a prominent and well-known business man of that city.

He was educated at the Albany Academy and Union College, being graduated A.B. in the class of 1832. Among his classmates were Alexander W. Bradford, afterwards Surrogate of New York County; Gilbert M. Speir, late Judge of the Superior Court, and Lieutenant-Governor David R. Floyd-Jones. After graduation he began the study of law in the office of McCown & Van Buren, in Albany, and upon his admission to the bar, became a partner of Mr. Van Buren, who, having been made Attorney-General, appointed him his deputy. The firm continued prominent at the bar of Albany until their removal in 1848 to New York City, where for the next ten years they were most active and successful.

Judge Robinson's experience as deputy and assistant to the Attorney-General gave him a practical knowledge of the law of corporations and municipalities which thereafter became his specialty in practice.

Among their first clients in New York was Edwin Forrest, whom they represented as attorneys in his famous twenty-year divorce suit.

After the termination of their partnership, Judge

Robinson carried on his practice alone for several years. In that time he acted as referee in numerous important cases and achieved a well-deserved popularity in that capacity. George Law and John Kerr, the railroad magnates, were his clients, and in connection with Charles O'Conor, he played an important part in the famous railroad cases which resulted in the notable decision in People *v.* Kerr, by which the Seventh Avenue, Broadway, and Dry Dock Railroads were enabled to construct their lines. He was counsel for these companies and others, and continued as referee in a vast number of important cases, which were referred to him by consent of parties, until his elevation to the bench.

In 1863, Mr. Robinson formed a co-partnership with Mr. John M. Scribner under the style of Robinson & Scribner, which was continued for seven years.

Mr. Robinson declined the Democratic nomination to the Judgeship of the Court of Appeals in 1870 in favor of his friend, Charles A. Rapallo, who was consequently elected; but, in the following May, accepted the nomination to the bench of the Court of Common Pleas, to which he was elected for a term of fourteen years and six months, beginning July 1, 1870.

As a practitioner, Judge Robinson was noted for his painstaking application to the details of a case, never going to trial with any cause until he had mastered every intricacy and provided against all contingencies and difficulties. He also made a thorough study of his clients' interests, and was thus enabled to advise them and provide for their particular needs and wishes as would a family physician for a patient. In his judicial capacity he showed deep legal scholarship, and the fairness and accuracy of his decisions were unquestioned so exhaustive and studied were they in every particular. He was particularly noted for his patience and urbanity and courtesy to all who approached him.

On the occasion of his death the bench and bar combined in sincere expression of their loss and in tributes to his memory at a special meeting called for that purpose on April 24, 1879. (See proceedings reported in 7 Daly Reports.) A commemorative tablet in his honor has been recently erected in the General Term room of the Court of Common Pleas, in the County Court House, New York, of which special mention will be found in another place. His portrait has hung on the walls in the same room since shortly after his death.

Judge Robinson was twice married, first to Emma Whitney, of Albany, N. Y., who died in 1865 at his country seat in Worcester, Otsego Co., N. Y.; and second to Mrs. Catherine D. Barker, of Albany, who survived him.

Judge Robinson died in New York City, April 7, 1879, leaving two sons and two daughters. One of his sons, Mr. Henry A. Robinson, is a practicing lawyer, and is the attorney for the Metropolitan Traction Company.

THE HONORABLE RICHARD LUDLOW
LARREMORE, LL.D.*

Richard Ludlow Larremore, sixteenth Judge of the Court of Common Pleas, was born near Astoria, L. I., on September 6, 1830, and died in this city on September 13, 1893. His descent in the maternal line was from the early Dutch settlers of New Netherland. On the paternal side his ancestry was English, but long resident on Long Island. He was graduated from Rutgers College in 1850.

He studied law with the firm of Betts & Robinson, and on his admission to the bar became a partner of Scoles and Cooper, who were leading members of the admiralty bar at that time. The law of real property was the branch to which young Larremore especially devoted his attention, and he soon became the counsel of the Dry Dock Savings Institution, and of other clients who made loans on real estate security. It may truthfully be said that he never lost a client, and that every client became his friend for life. The estimation in which he was held may be learned from the fact that he was frequently solicited to act as guardian and executor, positions that he firmly refused to accept.

---

* This memorial was prepared after Judge Larremore's death by his associate, Judge George M. Van Hoesen, and was read by Judge Van Hoesen at a meeting of The Association of the Bar of the City of New York, held on March 13, 1894.

RICHARD L. LARREMORE, LL.D.

A memorial of Chief Justice Larremore would be incomplete without a reference to his long and faithful service to the cause of public education. For many years he was an active member of the Board of Education, and for three years was president of the board. His firmness prevented that body from falling under the control of the Tweed Ring, and effectually stopped a bold attempt to apply to the purchase of school supplies the methods that obtained in the building of the County Court House.

In 1867 he was elected to the Constitutional Convention by a very flattering vote, and he took a prominent part in the debates, being especially well qualified to speak on all questions affecting our system of popular education.

In 1870, when the judicial force of the Court of Common Pleas was increased, he was elected to the bench of that Court in company with Hamilton W. Robinson and Joseph F. Daly. Charles H. Van Brunt, who had previously been appointed to fill a vacancy, was elected a Judge of the Common Pleas on the same ticket.

Judge Larremore left a large practice, which, though consisting largely of conveyancing, had been sufficiently varied to equip him for the duties on which he entered. His native quickness of apprehension and his ready command of resources soon gave him a recognized position as a *nisi prius* Judge; but in equity causes, for which his experience gave him special training, his judicial work was from the first of a high order.

He always had a well-defined sense of what the law ought to be when a novel question was suddenly raised. He had a good memory, not for the titles, but for the

essential principles of important cases, and it was his
habit to familiarize himself with the latest adjudications.
Though he was very fortunate in handling cases where
no opportunity for an examination of the authorities
was given to him, he welcomed the labor of research,
and shrank from no toil that a conscientious desire to
reach the very truth in the law involved.   His opinions were almost always brief, and though reversals fall
to the lot of every Judge he was exceptionally fortunate in the Appellate Court.

A good illustration of his judicial methods may be
found in his opinion in Dupré *vs*. Rein, 7 Abb. N. C.,
256.   That case involved an examination of the status
of a tripartite agreement between husband and wife with
the intervention of a trustee, entered into after the
separation of the wedded pair.   Citing many authorities he stated the existing rules regulating the recipro-
cal duties and liabilities of the parties and the methods
of enforcing them, with great conciseness, but with the
keenest discrimination.   That case has frequently been
cited and followed and has received the honor of special
mention by the Court of Appeals, an honor seldom falling to a decision at Special Term.

Though Chief Justice Larremore never trimmed his
sails to catch the breeze of popular favor he was
always a very popular man.   The courtesy and kindness that endeared him to the younger members of the
bar were the offspring of a genial nature that ever
manifested itself in his intercourse with the world, and
which won for him golden opinions from all.   He sat
in the Supreme Court by the order of the Governor,
and grew in reputation whilst an incumbent of that

bench. His associates, on the retirement of Chief Justice Charles P. Daly, chose him as the Chief Justice of the Court of Common Pleas. In 1869, the degree of LL.D. was conferred upon Judge Larremore by the University of the City of New York.

THE HONORABLE GEORGE M. VAN HOESEN.

Sprung from one of the oldest of our Dutch families, with a distinguished record as a soldier, no greater compliment could have been paid to the legal abilities of Judge George M. Van Hoesen, the seventeenth Judge of the Court of Common Pleas, than the general regret which was expressed by the prominent New York journals of all shades of political opinions, on his retirement from the bench in 1890.

Born in New York, he was graduated at the University of the City of New York. Prominent in many of the under-graduate organizations, he has since graduation served as president of the Alumni Association.

He studied law in the State and National Law School, then located at Poughkeepsie, and for a time was an instructor there on the subjects of pleadings and evidence. Going to Davenport, Iowa, shortly after, he began the practice of the law there, and so continued until the breaking out of the war in 1861 when, forming a company of which he was made captain, he was attached to the 13th Iowa Infantry. Serving under General Grant in Missouri, and ascending the Tennessee River with him in 1862, he was promoted to the rank of major for gallantry at the battle of Shiloh, and took part in the subsequent capture of Vicksburg. At one time he was provost-marshal of the armies in the

GEORGE M. VAN HOESEN.

field for the Department of the Mississippi. At the close of the war Major Van Hoesen resumed the practice of law in New York City, where his success was marked.

Perhaps the most notable event connected with Judge Van Hoesen's practice at this period was the fact that in 1866 he drew the first bill ever drawn for the construction of an elevated railway. Mr. Richard Montgomery had invented a plan for an aerial railway. Judge Van Hoesen interested capitalists in the enterprise, but considering the expression "aerial" a little flighty, caused the proposed law to be entitled, "An Act to Authorize the Construction of an Elevated Railway on Broadway," thus giving the name "elevated" to the system which is so well known to-day. The bill, which passed the Assembly by a large majority, failed in the Senate, but it was the pioneer of the legislation that has given to New York the nearest approach to rapid transit. Upon the retirement of Judge Van Hoesen, in 1889, an editorial in one of the leading metropolitan journals well expressed the dominant feeling at the time, calling it a misfortune "that a man of his talents, kindly feelings and dignified courtesy could not have received a renomination."

After leaving the bench Judge Van Hoesen resumed active practice. The same care, industry, accuracy, and conscientiousness which he exercised in the discharge of his judicial duties have ever marked his relations in regard to his clients. Possessed of a wonderful memory he is not only remarkably well versed in the principles of the law but can always quote his authorities with accuracy and promptness. Of kindly nature, gentle and pleasant in his manners, upright in all his relations to life, honors have come in abundance to Judge Van Hoesen. He is a trustee of the Holland Trust Company, was chairman for three successive terms of the Memorial Committee of the Grand Army, of which he has long been a comrade in La Fayette Post No. 140; was one of the founders and has been one of the presidents of the Holland Society. On the organization of the Zeta Psi Club, in 1882, he was by acclamation tendered its presidency. He is also a member of the Union and Manhattan Clubs, the St. Nicholas Society, and of the Historical and Geographical Societies.

Judge Van Hoesen is unmarried and is still engaged in the active practice of his profession.

MILES BEACH.

THE HONORABLE MILES BEACH.

More litigation came before the Supreme Court in the City of New York than was brought before either the Superior Court or the Court of Common Pleas. To relieve the Supreme Court Judges the Governor was accustomed to appoint one of the Judges of the Superior Court and one of the Judges of the Court of Common Pleas to sit on the Supreme Bench. Judge Miles Beach, through frequent appointments of successive Governors to act with the Justices of the Supreme Court, was always more identified in the popular mind with the latter than with the Court to which he had been originally appointed and twice elected and of which he was one of the last Judges.

Son of the late Hon. William A. Beach, who ranked with Charles O'Conor, James T. Brady, and other prominent lawyers of the preceding generation, Miles Beach, eighteenth Judge of the Court of Common Pleas, was born at Saratoga Springs in 1833. Soon after his graduation at Union College in 1854, he became associated with his father in the law firm of Messrs. Beach & Smith, at Troy, N. Y. The law business of this firm grew to such an extent that in 1871 father and son came to New York. Upon the election of Judge Rapallo to the Court of Appeals the law firm of Rapallo, Daly & Brown was changed to Beach, Daly & Brown, with the Messrs. Beach as members of the

119

firm.   Mr. Daly retiring, the firm became Beach &
Brown, and, acting as attorneys for Mr. Jay Gould
and for some of the Vanderbilts, had, for a period, the
largest railway business in New York.

In 1879, Governor Robinson appointed Mr. Beach
Justice of the Court of Common Pleas.   Though his
opponents in the election of the following year were
ex-Recorder Smyth and Elihu Root, he was elected in
the Autumn, and again re-elected at the end of his
term, in 1893, for another term of fourteen years.

Judge Beach has been known for many years as one
of the most cultivated Judges of the New York Courts.
His " opinions" are models of conciseness.   He has a
notable faculty of expressing his conclusions in half the
space usually required by others.

By the Constitution of 1894 Judge Beach was permanently transferred to the bench of the Supreme Court.

HENRY WILDER ALLEN.

THE HONORABLE HENRY WILDER ALLEN.

Henry Wilder Allen, nineteenth Judge of the Court of Common Pleas, was born at Alfred, Maine, October 18, 1833. He was a son of the Hon. William Cutter Allen, a lawyer by profession, and for many years Judge of Probate for York County, Maine; and the grandson on his maternal side, of Henry Holmes, a native of Kingston, Mass., a graduate of Brown University, and an active member of the bar for many years at Alfred, Maine.

Prepared for college at the schools of his native town he was duly graduated at Dartmouth College, New Hampshire, with the class of 1856.

While an under-graduate he became an active member in one of the more noted Greek fraternities, a fact which doubtless did much to develop those social qualities which rendered Judge Allen so popular in after life.

He taught in Alfred Academy for a little while after leaving college, but soon coming to New York became a clerk in the office of Hon. Nelson J. Waterbury. When the latter became District Attorney for the City of New York Mr. Allen followed his chief and became a clerk in the District Attorney's office. The friendship between the two men so ripened that when Judge Waterbury returned to private practice he and Mr. Allen became partners under the firm name of Waterbury & Allen, Mr. Allen in the meantime having been admitted to the bar.

Subsequently, through the recommendation of United States District Judge Samuel Blatchford, Mr. Allen was appointed by Chief Justice Salmon P. Chase, one of the registrars in bankruptcy in the City of New York. He filled this office so satisfactorily that upon the recommendation of Mr. Hubert O. Thompson he was appointed by Governor Cleveland, in 1884, Judge of the Court of the Common Pleas of the City of New York. In the following Autumn he was elected for the full term of fourteen years.

Popular, well educated, a good companion, he was in all his dealings noted for his scrupulous honesty. Exact in his own relations with those with whom he was brought in contact, he compelled the same exactitude in his subordinates. Possessed of a thorough knowledge of details as well as of human nature and of the niceties of life, he served for many years as Chairman of the House Committee of the Manhattan Club with great satisfaction, not only to those who knew him personally, but to the entire membership of that institution.

While leaving the Court House, he was seized with a paralytic stroke, and his untimely death at the Chambers Street Hospital, after several days' illness, in 1891, cut him off in the full plentitude of his powers.

HENRY W. BOOKSTAVER, LL.D.

THE HONORABLE HENRY W. BOOKSTAVER, LL.D.

Henry W. Bookstaver, twentieth Judge of the Court of Common Pleas, was born in Orange County, New York, in 1835. He is the son of Daniel Bookstaver and a direct descendant of Jacobus Buchstabe, or Boochstaber, who emigrated from Switzerland early in the eighteenth century and became an extensive owner of real estate in Orange County. The original form of the family name signifies "book-stick," a wooden letter such as was first used in printing—or denotes one engaged in the printing of books. The family was a noted one in the old country; two brothers, Henry and Johannes Buchstabe, being prominent on opposite sides in the theological struggles of the middle of the sixteenth century. It is from Henry, who espoused the reformed religion, that the Judge is descended.

Judge Bookstaver was graduated with honors at Rutgers College, New Brunswick, N. J., in 1859, and immediately entered the office of Brown, Hall & Vanderpoel. He was admitted to the bar in 1861, and shortly afterwards was taken as a partner into the firm with which he had studied.

He became successively sheriff's attorney, counsel to the Police Board, and counsel to the Commissioners of Charities and Corrections. His defence of Sheriff Reilly established his reputation, not so much for legal acumen—for he already had that—as for forensic eloquence. In 1885 he was raised to the bench by a large plurality over Judge Paterson and Theron G. Strong. During twenty-five years at the bar he enjoyed an extensive practice covering all branches of the law, and had acquired a perfect familiarity with every question likely to arise at a trial term. He has also been keenly interested in the study of scientific and general topics of interest; being a member of the Archæological, Historical and Geographical Societies of New York City; of the Metropolitan Museum of Art and the American Museum of Natural History; the Botanical Garden Society and various other scientific and literary organizations. His training was, therefore, such as has come to few of our Judges, and his ability as a trial Judge is reckoned among the highest on the bench of New York Courts. He is noted for the clearness of his methods of presenting facts, his power to inspire confidence and his unfailing courtesy.

Socially, Judge Bookstaver enjoys wide popularity, and is a member of the Manhattan, Casino, New York and Zeta Psi Clubs, and of the St. Nicholas and Huguenot Societies, all of New York City. He is a member of the governing body of the Dutch Reformed Church, the second richest religious corporation in the city.

The degree of LL.D. was conferred on him by Rutgers College in 1888.

He was married in 1865 to Miss Mary Baily Young, daughter of Charles Young, of Hamptonburg, Orange County, N. Y.

By the Constitution of 1894 Judge Bookstaver was transferred to the bench of the Supreme Court.

HENRY BISCHOFF, JR.

THE HONORABLE HENRY BISCHOFF, Jr.

Henry Bischoff, Jr., twenty-first Judge of the Court of Common Pleas, was born in 1852 in the City of New York. Nearly one hundred years ago, his paternal grandfather was a church builder in Germany, but subsequently engaged in the business of a lumber merchant and brick manufacturer at Achim in the kingdom of Prussia, where his descendants still carry on the business he established. His father, Mr. Henry Bischoff, has been a banker in the city of New York for upwards of forty-nine years.

The son entered his father's office, but later determined upon a professional career. He read law, was graduated at the Columbia College Law School in 1871, and at the same time secured "honorable mention" from the Department of Political Science. Being at graduation but nineteen years of age, he was not admitted to the bar till November, 1873, when, devoting himself to civil causes, he succeeded so well that in June, 1889, he became the attorney to the Tax Department, and in the following November, 1890, was elected a Judge of the Court of Common Pleas.

Judge Bischoff is a director of the Oratorio Society, and of the Union Square Bank. He is a member of the German Society, the New York State and American Bar Associations, the Manhattan and Democratic

Clubs, and the Liederkranz, Arion, Beethoven and Mænnerchor Societies.

His moral courage, his self reliance, his independence of character, his firm adherence to the right cause have rendered his decisions more than usually acceptable to the bar. Though one of the youngest Judges on the bench, he has already become noted for his industry, his uniform courtesy, and the soundness of his decisions. Judge Bischoff was married in October, 1873, to Miss Annie Louise Moshier, daughter of Frederick and Louise Moshier. They have one child, a daughter, Loula, born May 13, 1876. Transferred by the Constitution of 1894 to the Supreme Court, he, together with Judges Joseph F. Daly and McAdam, composes the Appellate Term which hears all appeals from the decisions of the lower Courts.

ROGER A. PRYOR, LL.D.

THE HONORABLE ROGER A. PRYOR, LL.D.

Roger Atkinson Pryor, twenty-second Judge of the Court of Common Pleas, editor, diplomat, statesman and soldier, son of the Rev. Theodoric Pryor, who was known for over half a century as an eloquent and eminent Presbyterian clergyman, was born in Dinwiddie County, Virginia, in 1828. He was graduated at Hampden-Sidney College, took several schools at the University of Virginia; was admitted to the bar; entered journalism, was editor of the *Southside Democrat* at Petersburg, of the *Washington Union*, and of the *Richmond Enquirer;* was appointed in 1855 on a special mission to Greece by President Pierce, and, on his return in 1856, attracted great attention through his opposition to Mr. William L. Yancey's plans for the re-opening of the slave trade. He was elected to the National Congress in 1857, and re-elected in 1859. Upon the secession of his State, he became a member of the provisional Confederate Congress and subsequently of the first regular Confederate Congress. He was in turn colonel, brigadier-general and private, for when political reasons had induced him to resign his commission as brigadier-general, he immediately re-enlisted as a private in the Confederate army. Taken prisoner in 1864, he was confined in Fort Lafayette.

After the war, Gen. Pryor removed to New York, determined to devote himself to the legal profession.

127

He was obliged, however, to begin his studies anew, and was at the time thirty-five years of age, without fortune, having the responsibility of a large family, and settled among strangers.

While studying law, he supported his family, by writing for the press. Admitted to practice he soon became recognized in the profession. He was engaged in some of the most important causes of the time, including the Beecher trial, the Elevated Railroad cases, the divorce suit of Governor Sprague, of Rhode Island, and was of counsel with Gen. Butler in all the Sprague Estate litigations, and also in the suit in the United States Circuit Court to recover the New York & New England Railroad for its original stockholders. Gen. Pryor defended Governor Ames on his impeachment by the Legislature of Mississippi. In the controversy between Mr. Tilton and Mr. Beecher, Gen. Pryor was retained by the former. He made the argument before the General Term of the City Court, and before the Court of Appeals, resisting the granting to the defendant of a bill of particulars as well as the argument before Judge Neilson in favor of the competency of Mr. Tilton as a witness, In both these contests, Gen. Pryor was opposed by Mr. William M. Evarts and his arguments gave him celebrity as a profound and accomplished lawyer.

The honors conferred upon Gen. Pryor, were culminated when he was appointed in the latter part of 1890 by Governor Hill to the bench of the Common Pleas, and this was made the occasion of a remarkable compliment in the form of a banquet at the Astor House, New York, given in Judge Pryor's honor by the Hon. John Russell Young. At this banquet were assembled about fifty guests, including President Cleveland, Chauncey M. Depew, judges, lawyers, clergymen, eminent physicians, prominent merchants, military men, editors of all creeds and of all stripes of political belief, thus rendering a magnificent testimonial to the position in New York which Judge Pryor had reached in the face of the most pronounced obstacles, and while combating conditions which might reasonably have defeated his ambition and his hope.

Perhaps one of the most curious facts concerning Judge Pryor is that his legal, political and military record have overshadowed the position to which his scholastic training entitles him. A man of thought as well as a man of action, he stood at the head of his class when he was graduated at Hampden-Sidney in 1845, and has since, some ten years ago, received from his Alma Mater the highest honor which she could give, the degree of Doctor of Laws. The University of Virginia, which has never granted honorary degrees, has made him one of her Board of Visitors. Elected in November, 1890, for the full term of fourteen years, Judge Pryor was, by the Constitution of 1894, transferred in 1896 to the bench of the Supreme Court.

THE HONORABLE LEONARD A. GIEGERICH.

Leonard A. Giegerich, twenty-third Judge of the Court of Common Pleas, was born in Rotz, Bavaria, May 20th, 1855, and was brought to this country when scarcely more than one year old. He was educated at the public schools, the St. Nicholas parochial school and the De La Salle Institute, N. Y., but from the age of twelve he was obliged to earn his own livelihood. He studied law and was admitted to the bar in 1877. He was elected to the State Assembly in 1886, and in 1887 was appointed by President Cleveland Collector of Internal Revenue for the Third New York District. Governor Hill in 1890, appointed him to a vacancy on the City Court Bench, caused by the death of Judge Nehrbas. Though it was generally thought that Judge Giegerich would receive the Democratic nomination for the full term as City Court Judge, political exigencies decreed differently. It was deemed wise to strengthen the local ticket among the Germans. Judge Giegerich again in 1890, and much against his will, was nominated and elected County Clerk. He held this office, one of the most remunerative in the Courts, until the following Autumn, when he resigned to accept the appointment by Governor Hill to fill a vacancy on the bench of the Court of Common Pleas caused by the sudden death of Judge Allen. Both political parties placed him in nomination in 1892, to succeed himself,

LEONARD A. GIEGERICH.

and he was elected for the full term of fourteen years. He was also elected a member of the recent Constitutional Convention.

As a member of Assembly, his record was warmly endorsed by the Reform Club of New York. He was one of the two members who persistently refused all passes from railway corporations.

As County Clerk he introduced many reforms which relieved wants long felt by practicing lawyers. During his incumbency of the County Clerkship, he endeared himself, probably without the least intention, to all historians by the classifying of musty records, 200 years old that had been stored for years in the Court House.

Always attentive to duty, he has required the same attention from those under him, and has thus earned the reputation of a disciplinarian.

Though the youngest Judge on the Common Pleas Bench, his record was most satisfactory to both the bar and the public, and he has rapidly acquired a reputation as one of the best trial Judges of our time.

Judge Giegerich was married in 1887 to Miss Louise M. Boll, of New York City, and they have had several children.

By the Constitution of 1894 Judge Giegerich was transferred to the Supreme Court.

THE NEW ORGANIZATION OF THE COURT OF COMMON PLEAS, JULY 1, 1870.

The amended New York State Constitution of 1869 provided for the election of three additional Judges of the Court of Common Pleas. In pursuance of this provision, Hamilton W. Robinson, Joseph F. Daly and Richard L. Larremore were chosen as such Judges at the election in the city of New York held in May, 1869.

According to the statute they were to enter upon the duties of their office on the first of July, 1870. The oath of office was administered to them at noon. The ceremony took place in the large room of the trial term, Part I. of the Common Pleas. At the appointed hour all the seats and standing places were occupied, mainly by Judges and members of the bar.

Among those who occupied seats upon the platform, in addition to the Common Pleas Judges, were Judge Woodruff, of the United States Court; Judges Bosworth, Mitchell, Henry E. Davies, late Chief Justice of the Court of Appeals; Pierrepont, Slosson, Vanvorst, Judge Brady, of the Supreme Court; Messrs. Chas. O'Conor, Peter Cooper, Smith Barker, J. W. Gerard, Judges Jones, Fithian and Freedman, of the Superior Court; Henry Nicoll, N. J. Waterbury and Wm. M. Evarts. Among those present beside these, were notably: Messrs. Luther R. Marsh, Augustus F. Smith, A. J.

Vanderpoel, Algernon S. Sullivan, Henry Brewster, Jesse K. Furlong, Frank Byrne, Amos G. Hull, Henry Morrison, Mr. Devine, Wm. H. Ingersoll, D. Marvin, J. M. Scribner, Wm. Edelsten, Dennis McMahon, Frederick Smythe, Clarence A. Seward, Mr. Pinckney, Mr. Spink and Justice Quinn.

Chief Justice Chas. P. Daly administered the usual oath of office to the three new Judges severally, after which he announced that in consequence of the additional number of Judges in that Court, some alterations had been made in the rules, which would be made known to the bar in due time.

ADDRESS OF MR. J. W. GERARD.

Mr. James W. Gerard then addressed the audience at some length. He had, he said, never been a Judge; no politician or lawyer had ever thought of making him one, though why he did not know. He had for a long time believed that he possessed some of the attributes of a Judge. The speaker gave a history of the Court of Common Pleas, from the time when, more than 200 years ago, this same Court was known as the Court of the Mayor, Aldermen and Sheriff of New Amsterdam. This Court was the oldest one in the State. Peter Stuyvesant was one of the first Judges. In that day the Court was always opened with prayer. (The speaker here read the prayer used upon such occasions and pronounced it to be a model prayer in its simplicity and purity of thought.) In those days they did what we have finally concluded to do—that is, allow all parties to be witnesses for themselves in both civil and criminal cases. They had juries then, but the Dutchmen

133

did not like that system much, and generally preferred to have their causes heard before a Judge. Peter Stuyvesant, he said, authorized the first fee bill in New York. His doctrine was that lawyers should "serve the poor gratis for God's sake." We make it up in charging the rich man. Within a hundred yards of the Court House, Mr. Gerard said, he had seen a man tied to the whipping post and whipped according to a judicial decision, for an offense committed in the post-office. Sometimes they put the offenders in the stocks and threw rotten eggs at them. In 1665, the name was changed to the Mayor's Court, and so continued for about 160 years, or until about the year 1821, when it was altered to the Court of Common Pleas. The speaker recited a long list of names of those who had occupied seats on the bench of the Common Pleas, and also those who were prominent practioners at its bar. Among them he mentioned DeWitt Clinton, the father of the Erie Canal; Cadwallader Colden, Col. Willett, Samuel Jones, the grandfather of a Judge now on the Superior Court Bench; Matthew Livingston, Pierre C. Van Wyck, Josiah Ogden Hoffman, Richard Riker, John T. Irving, brother of Washington Irving, the poet; Martin S. Wilkins, Elisha W. King, Gen. Robert Bogardus, David Graham, Jr., and John Leveridge. The address of Mr. Gerard was delivered in his usually humorous vein, and was frequently relieved by anecdotes.

ADDRESS OF MR. AUGUSTUS F. SMITH.

Mr. A. F. Smith spoke of the Court of Common Pleas, since he commenced to practice in it, a little more than a quarter of a century ago.   The bar must recollect that this Court, during the last quarter of a century, was a very different tribunal from what it was during the times of which Mr. Gerard had spoken.   In those early days, there was only one Judge.   The Court could not be held more than two days at one term, nor could there be more than four terms in a year, and only eight attorneys were allowed to practice in the Court. He spoke of Judge Irving, who for seventeen years was a Judge of this Court, and who for fourteen years of that time was the sole Judge.   He did not propose to compare him with his brother, Washington Irving. What lawyer was there whose name will be known in future generations except in the way of anecdote and legend?   At the meeting of the bar recently held in regard to the death of Mr. F. B. Cutting, he heard it stated that the deceased owed his great success to friends and family influence, who enabled him suddenly to reach the height of his profession.   The speaker wished to say to the young members of the bar that he did not believe any man ever achieved success at the bar by means of friends.   Something was undoubtedly due to circumstances, but it must be by honesty, industry, perseverance, and a faithful discharge of duty to clients, that any success worth retaining can be attained in the legal profession.

Mr. Luther R. Marsh was the next and last speaker.

ADDRESS OF MR. LUTHER R. MARSH.

I suppose I may consider myself commissioned to unite with the gentlemen who have spoken, in virtue of having represented the first cause which appears in the regular series of the reported cases in this Court—a cause in which no one else survives of the parties, attorneys, counsel or witnesses, though only fifteen years have since elapsed. The people of the State of New York, as well as of the city, let us hope, have good cause to congratulate themselves on the changes just wrought in their judicial system by the amended Constitution. Among them, the lengthened tenure of office is a decided improvement—reaching, as now established, to about half a generation—more than half of what may fairly be considered the average business life of man. This makes the judgeship a sort of life-work; and while Judges are men, with considerable human nature in them, it must necessarily induce a feeling of greater security and a more absolute independance of judgment. Among these changes, the new features engrafted upon this Court of Common Pleas for the City and County of New York—by which its numerical power is doubled—and it, no longer dependent on legislative will, has struck the flukes of its anchor into the Constitution itself. The ceremony we witness this day is one of great significance. It is not merely the usual result of an election; filling important offices either with former incumbents or a new personality. It is not the retirement of certain men from judicial stations they had occupied, and the advance of other men to supply the vacancy. If it were that, and only that, it would be an imposing ceremony. The smooth and peaceful change of power, from hand to hand, is, of itself, a sublime event. The advent of a new priest at the altar; of a new representative of justice; of one who is to stand with absolute

impartiality, between contending litigants; who is to
see that wantonness and selfishness do not override
justice and right, to hold, with steady nerve, those hal-
lowed scales, which shall weigh to each applicant his
due, and shall pronounce all forms of injustice, wanting,
in the balance; to guard the doctrines settled by the
Courts, so that uniformity shall be maintained, and
men may know the standard by which their rights and
duties are to be squared, to enforce the will of the
whole people as expressed in the enactments of their
Legislature—such an inauguration is an event ever to
be regarded with interest. But this is all that, and
something more. It is an enlargement of the altar
itself. It is, in effect, adding a new Court of equal
power and jurisdiction to the one already existing. It
is launching anew with enlarged capacities, and age
renewed, this ancient and most useful Court, the oldest
judicial tribunal in our State, which begun its life of
toil and duty, though under another name, two hundred and five years ago, this just retreating month of
June; which saw this great city of ours in its struggling
youth, and whose roots are deep and firm in the primal
soil of our own liberty. An interesting epoch, therefore, in the history of this Court, do we behold this day.
Of the many changes of added or diminished function
which have occurred in its organization during the last
two centuries, this is not the least. But though it
enters this day on a new career—let us believe for yet
other centuries to come—and though most of the present and now newly inaugurated ministers of its power
are untried to its bench, though not to its bar, yet does
not, nor will this tribunal seem strange to its habitual

practioners, as long as he, who is more intimately identified with the Court than any of his predecessors, and to whom we are indebted for the biography of the Court itself, continues to be a participant in its authority. Of those who have enunciated the law from this seat, some have departed to the Grand Assize: Edward Livingston, De Witt Clinton, Jacob Radcliffe, Col. Marinus Willett, Cadwallader D. Colden, John T. Irving and William Inglis. Others have been transferred to other tribunals, where they are now at work: Michael Ulshoeffer, to the quiet but efficient administration of the Referee's office; Daniel P. Ingraham, Albert Cardozo and John R. Brady to the Supreme Court; and Lewis B. Woodruff, first to the Superior Court, then to the Court of Appeals, and now to the Federal Judiciary; while yet others, Henry Hilton, Hooper C. Van Vorst, and George C. Barrett, have returned to the forum, to invoke the very powers they wielded from its bench. But the Presiding Judge remains faithful to his first love; and that familiar form, which, for twenty-six years, has occupied this bench may be seen there still. Let it be our prayer and hope that this honorable Court, venerable by its days, but fresh in its vigor, may ever boast as able and upright Judges in the coming years, as in the past, and preserve its ermine as immaculate, that it may still hold in order the surging interests of this commercial community, and that it may continue to rear and educate advocates in its arena, who, like Emmet, Jay and Samson, of a former day, and, more recently, like Brady, so lately gone, and Cutting, yesterday laid at his rest, shall add to its usefulness, its honor and its renown.

PROCEEDINGS ON THE DEATH OF JUDGE HAMILTON W. ROBINSON, APRIL 24, 1879.

The next proceedings of any especial moment on the part of the bar of the City and County of New York in connection with the Court of Common Pleas, took place on Thursday, April 24, 1879, at the Court House New York City. On that day a meeting of the bench and bar was held to commemorate the life and services of the Honorable Hamilton W. Robinson, who died April 7, 1879, during his term of office as Judge of the Court. Chief Justice Charles P. Daly presided over the meeting. The vice-presidents were the Honorables Noah Davis, George C. Barrett, Gilbert M. Speir, John Sedgwick, William G. Choate, John K. Porter, Stephen D. Law, John R. Brady, A. R. Lawrence, Hooper C. Van Vorst, J. J. Freedman, Charles O'Conor, William A. Beach, Charles Donohue, William E. Curtis, Charles F. Sanford, Samuel Blatchford, David Dudley Field, Lucien Birdseye.

The secretaries were: Messrs. John M. Scribner, James J. Thomson, Douglass Campbell and James T. Law.

Resolutions eulogizing Judge Robinson were passed at the meeting and ordered to be entered on the minutes of the Court. Addresses were made by Messrs. A. J. Vanderpoel, Luther R. Marsh; by ex-Judge Lucien Birdseye and Judges Hooper C. Van Vorst and Charles P. Daly.

We have met to pay respect to the memory of the late Hamilton W. Robinson. While this tribute is due to his character as a lawyer and as a Judge, it is also a tribute and token of our respect and affection for him as a man.

For nine years he has been a member of the bench of the Court of Common Pleas of the City and County of New York. Thirty years of hard labor and varied practice at the bar had thoroughly fitted him for this position, from which an all-wise Providence has removed him in the prime of life and season of usefulness. He was justly noted for the patient study and careful preparations of his cases, and every question likely to arise was fully investigated and brought to the test of his well-balanced mind. In his bearing he was diffident and unobtrusive; in his friendships, cordial and sincere. As a Judge he always remembered "that a Judge must never be allow himself to be warped or trammelled, and must ever maintain the free employment of a watchful and unbiased mind."

Mr. Vanderpoel then offered the following resolutions:

Resolved, That by the death of Judge Hamilton W. Robinson, we have lost one who was an honor to the judiciary and to our profession. His urbanity of manner while at the bar and on the bench, his sincerity of heart and faithfulness to duty had endeared him to us; while his learning, probity and justice command for him universal respect. We cherish pleasant recollections of his well-spent life, and revere his memory as an able and upright Judge.

LUTHER R. MARSH.

Resolved, That the proceedings of this meeting be presented to the Court of which Judge Robinson was a member, with the request that they be entered upon its minutes.

ADDRESS OF MR. LUTHER R. MARSH.

MR. PRESIDENT:—In rising to second the resolutions presented by Mr. Vanderpoel, which so truly deplore our loss, a few additional words may not be out of place.

So rapid are the changes in our bar; such a tide of new practitioners is constantly poured into it from all sections of the nation, that there are many here, no doubt, who have only known him—whose loss has called us together—in his office as a Judge.

There are some present—among them his class-mates Judge Speir and Samuel Campbell—whose memories hold the slender form of a beaming and studious youth at college; ambitious of honor, free from any evil habits, and on terms of cheerful amity with all his co-collegiates.

Some, too, here, remember him, when afterwards graduated from college, and from a counsellor's office, he had taken rank as a lawyer at Albany, where there were centered many men famous in the records of the bar.

Some too, remember him when, seeking a wider field, he encountered the hazards of a removal to this city, where only courage, effort and pertinacity could secure a foothold, and by his modest sign announced that he would give his time and labor to those who should intrust their interests to his hands.

He returned, temporarily, to Albany to officiate as deputy attorney-general under Mr. Van Buren; and, subsequently, they united in partnership, and so for many years continued in New York, where a clientage, large in volume and responsible in character and amount, grew up around them; numbering in its list George Law, and the great and varied interests he controlled.

The services of almost every lawyer are, at one time or another, called into use as a mutually selected arbiter; and for this Judge Robinson developed such a special adaptation that he became, and was several years, our most active and prominent referee—thus becoming especially educated to the duties of the office he was subsequently to fill. The proportion of causes disposed of by referees is very large; and they are often of the most troublesome and complex kind, involving many-itemed accounts, which a jury cannot try. The referee unites in himself the functions of juror and Judge; and, but for him, I do not see how the Courts could keep abreast of the accumulated business of the time. Of these referees, as I have said, Judge Robinson was, in his day, the most conspicuous; and such quantities of references flocked to his office, either by mutual consent or the compulsory orders of the Courts, that he might often be seen presiding at the trial of two, three, and even four causes at the same time—walking through his ample rooms to the various tables, and disposing of questions of pleading and evidence as he passed.

Judge Robinson, when he came to the bench, had well withstood the strain of his professional labors. He was, I believe, in perfect health. It is a question

of some moment whether, if he had remained at the
bar, he would not now have been living and in full
capacity. So many of our judiciary have become
impaired in health, that it suggests a very serious
inquiry as to the cause. Comes the trouble from the
over-breathed air of crowded rooms, or from the perpetual and unrelieved stress of judicial duties—peculiarly responsible and exhausting—or from the joint
effect of both ?

And yet it would not seem to be safe to deduce any
general principle from a limited range of facts; for on
that very bench in which this sad vacancy occurs, there
presides a jurist who has administered at its shrine for
more than a generation; who has carried on besides,
immense concurrent labors; who has gathered and
recorded the annals of that historic Court; who has
been ever ready to take part in all public meetings and
aid in all public enterprises; who, by his wise devotion to geographic science, has made his name familiar and respected over the world, and yet, who still
bears the evidence of health undiminished and vigor
unimpaired.

It was a pernicious habit—induced by his sensitively
nervous organization and the anxieties of his office—
which used to drive our departed friend, at midnight,
from his bed to his table, when many of his opinions
were written and revised. He must possess a large
original stock of vitality whose constitution can long
sustain the drafts upon it required by the intense and
varied application of the daytime in our city practice,
and carry protracted labor into the night besides. An

habitual encroachment on the domain and jurisdiction of

"Tired Nature's sweet restorer—balmy sleep,"

is, sooner or later, sure to be avenged.

He was a faithful and concentrate worker. But notwithstanding the remarkable facility with which he wrote, he used to revise and re-revise till his manuscript opinions almost required a Champollion to decipher them. I have been reminded, sometimes, while puzzling over his manuscripts, of a paper I saw when a student at Utica. There was, in the office of the late Charles A. Mann, a chest of historical documents left by Richard Varick. Amongst them, a draft petition to Congress, by Baron Steuben, for some additional aid, as I remember it. It was in the handwriting of Alexander Hamilton—whose pellucid style vindicates his renown as a writer—from whom, by the way, our late friend derived a portion of his name—and its erasures and interlineations evinced that it was not struck off at white heat, and at a blow; that it did not drop without labor from the nibs of the pen; but had received many a careful revision and correction.

It was, however, in his social relations—in the company of his family and friends—that Robinson was king. His supremacy there was affectionately acknowledged. It is believed that he never lost a friend; rather, he bound them to him with enduring cords. Some of his boyhood and college classmates have kept up with him, through the vicissitudes of life, the most intimate relations; and we may only witness the afflicting sorrow they express, to know how supremely he reigned in the domain of the affections.

His great pleasure was to spend the Summers on his ancestral acres at Worcester, in the County of Otsego, where he dispensed a charming and bountiful hospitality. He dreamed in his illness that the crisp air of the Otsego hills—resinous with the delicious odor of the woods—would renew his strength, like the eagle's; and that could he but touch his mother earth, he would, Antæus-like, receive new vigor in his frame. But he had approached too near the confine for any natural means to bring him back. And so, his mission here ended, he has gone to join the generations on the other side of the line; where our friends, in large majority, already are; the ultimate destination and home of all.

ADDRESS OF EX-JUDGE LUCIEN BIRDSEYE.

MR. CHAIRMAN AND GENTLEMEN:—My long acquaintance with Judge Robinson, the kindness with which he welcomed me to the ranks of the profession, and the earnest regard which was the fruit of my long intercourse with him, render it a privilege to me, painful indeed but real, to join in these tributes to his memory.

When I commenced practice in Albany, Mr. Robinson had been some years at the bar. Although, while there, he had been but the junior member of his firm—that of MacKown, Van Buren & Robinson—he had already made his mark as a lawyer. Mr. MacKown was Recorder of Albany. Presiding as he did at the monthly sessions of his Court, and feeling the burdens of his great age and increasing infirmity, he had substantially withdrawn from active participation in the business of the firm. The tastes and aptitudes of Mr.

Van Buren led him to engage in the contests of the bar and of the political arena, rather than in the severe studies and what to so many seem the dry labors of the law office; while these were precisely adapted to the tastes, and called forth all the powers of Mr. Robinson. Thus the business of the firm had passed at an early day into the hands of Mr. Robinson.

He, however, left that firm, and came to New York to engage in practice. I think his residence here at that period was too brief to do much more than prove his sagacity in selecting the field of his life's labors, and the real strength of character which underlaid all his modesty and self-distrust. For, without both sagacity and force of will, he would not have ventured into such a field.

When Mr. Van Buren was chosen attorney-general he induced Mr. Robinson to return to Albany to act as his chief assistant in that office, while he himself became still more completely the popular advocate and orator.

Taking up also the business of his former firm, the preparation of pleadings, opinions and briefs fully occupied his time, and led him far and wide in legal studies and examinations. At this period of his life, and indeed for many years afterwards, he was but rarely seen, and still more rarely heard in the Courts.

The bar of Albany was then a very strong one. Among those most frequently seen and heard in the Courts, and who were famous throughout the State and beyond it, were, besides Mr. Van Buren himself, such men as Samuel Stevens, Marcus T. Reynolds, Daniel Cady, Teunis Van Vechten, Nicholas Hill, Rufus W.

Peckham, Azor Taber, Julius Rhoades, Deodatus Wright, Henry C. Wheaton, Samuel H. Hammond and others.

But besides these men, famous as advocates and orators, there was then in Albany, as there must be at every bar, a class of men marked by characteristics very different.

Of retiring dispositions, distrusting themselves in the active contests before Courts and juries, hardly becoming accustomed or willing to hear their own voices, but yet knowing well their own powers of study and examination and logical statement, they gave themselves up to the labors of the office and library, rather than of the Court room. They made the deep researches into legal principles; prepared the careful array of authorities, and made the thorough preparations for trials and arguments, which, after all, are the real ground of professional success.

Among the men of this class were Gideon Hawley, Cyrus Stevens, George W. Peckham, Peter Cagger, Stephen D. Van Schaick our late lamented Surrogate in this city; Mr. Robinson and others. Some of these men, either by the native force of their character, or under the pressure of circumstances, as when the advocate of the firm had fallen, or been laid aside, overcame the modesty of their natures, and became useful and successful in the more active and public uses of the Courts.

Eminent as the bar of Albany then was for the ability and eloquence of its leading advocates, it may well be doubted whether it was not equally strong in the learning, the industry, the acuteness, the skill and the vigilance of those who, according to the English classification of our profession, would have been known only as attorneys and solicitors.

Such men as Mr. Cagger, Mr. Van Schaick and Mr. Robinson, were powers, not only in their several offices, but in the Courts, where they seldom appeared, and even in general business and public affairs. Each performed great labors and discharged with success great responsibilities. If, as has sometimes been the fact, the public, not knowing whose were the real labors that contributed so much to the triumphs of the bar, gave the fame and reputation to those whose voices had been heard there, rather than to those who had, in fact, but in private, done so much both to deserve and to command those successes, it was not strange. I am sure that none of the gentlemen I have named ever experienced a pang of disappointment, or felt anything but the desire to accomplish, in their several spheres, all that was possible to protect and promote the rights and interests of their clients.

Soon after the close of Mr. Van Buren's term of office as attorney-general, he and Mr. Robinson removed to this city. Here Mr. Robinson, though still disinclined to appear in the Court room, became well, if not widely, known for his great learning, his quick perceptions, his instant grasp of the points of a case, his logic, his power of legal statement; in short, for all that marks the lawyer and the judge.

As a consequence, he was sought as a referee. It was not at all the patronage of Judges, but the free choice of attorneys and parties, that made his offices to resemble rather a crowded Court room than the chambers of a very modest, quiet and retiring member of the profession.

Scarcely had Mr. Van Buren retired from active practice when those engaged in the litigated business of this city seemed to discover, as by common consent, that here was a great lawyer and a great Judge ready at their hand. The labors and studies of his early life had borne their fruit. And some years later, when this Court was reorganized, this verdict of the profession was ratified by that of the people, and he was placed on the bench of this Court.

In what manner he discharged the duties of his high office needs not be told in this place or this presence. On his own part, with what assiduity and faithfulness; with what fulness of learning; with what wide research; with what quickness of perception; with what patience; with what gentleness of demeanor and kindness of heart; with what singleness of mind and simple purpose to perform every day the duties of that day; and on the part of others, with what genuine, universal confidence in his uprightness, his purity, his unselfishness, his supreme love of right and truth and justice, I do not attempt to speak. For are not all these things recorded in all that he has done in this Court, and engraven on the memory of us all?

Let me, rather, say a few words of his personal character, as it impressed itself upon me during a friendship of many years.

It was my good fortune to become his friend at the very beginning of my own professional life; to have seen much of him while we dwelt in Albany; to have followed him thence to New York at an early day, and

in no small part because of his advice; to have had my
own chambers, for some years thereafter, almost in
common with his own; and during that time, and
always afterwards, to have regarded him with affection
and esteem.

Few men were better adapted to inspire esteem or
affection.

The same qualities of the mind and the heart which
seemed to withhold him from the forum made him
delightful as a companion. Genial, quick, ready,
keenly appreciating wit and humor, as ready and as
strong in conversation as in the use of the pen, sincere,
simple in tastes and pleasures, of a memory quick,
ready and correct, how could he be other than he was—
the charming companion, the friend, faithful, trusting
and trusted, loving and beloved?

That trait which has to me seemed, perhaps, the
most noteworthy in the character of our departed
brother, was the quickness, the clearness, the direct-
ness of every operation of his mind and heart. What
with others was a process, with him seemed oftentimes
to be a result. What other minds sought by induc-
tion, and with pains and labor, he appeared often to
reach as if at a glance. And this quickness and purity
of his mental operations was joined with, if not in large
part derived from, the quickness and purity of all the
feelings of his heart. His sympathies were ready. He
was himself last in his own thoughts. And so he was
considerate of the rights and interests, the enjoyments
and pleasures of all around him.

In reviewing the career now closed, so long, so full
of honor, and of all useful service, public and private,

one is, I think, reminded of a somewhat similar career, long since passed into the history of our profession.

It is now a little more than a hundred years since an English lawyer was promoted to the Court of the King's Bench, where he was long the associate and friend of Lord Mansfield, who desired him to be his own successor as Chief Justice. When Francis Buller was made Judge in the highest common law Court of England, it is said that the propriety of his appointment was questioned, because of his want of prominence and success as an advocate at the bar. But he adorned the bench of that Court for nearly a quarter of a century. He proved to be, almost, as it were, by nature and instinct, a great jurist, a great *nisi prius* lawyer, a great Judge. His book upon the practice at *nisi prius* was the first effort to state in a formal or scientific manner the principles of that part of the science of our profession. It has done much, especially in the writers whom he has led to treat of the same subject, to throw light upon what was in his day a very obscure, and must ever be a very important and difficult branch of practice.

Certainly it cannot be said that the elevation of Judge Robinson to the bench was anything like the experiment which the appointment of Mr. Justice Buller was at first thought by some to be, but which resulted so happily. For, at the time of his nomination and election, Judge Robinson (almost unknown as he was in the more active walks of his profession) had really passed through a more careful professional and judicial training than was at all known to or appreciated by most of his brothers at the bar. His whole career upon the bench has shown how his great natural powers had been disciplined and supplemented, by long and deep study and large experience, to fit him for his eminence as a lawyer and a Judge.

Still, it seems to me, that in the tone and character of their minds; in the amplitude and readiness of their learning; in their fitness for judicial labors; in their fondness for and faithfulness in those duties; and in the ease and clearness of their legal statements, these two great Judges were very much alike.

Indeed, I think it may be said, that in respect of all those qualities which render a lawyer and a Judge really useful and great, Judge Robinson was singularly well endowed.

Happy was he that in his life he secured so much of the respect and the love of all who came within the sphere of his influence; and that, at his death, he is found to deserve so well the admiration of those who shall come after him.

ADDRESS OF JUDGE HOOPER C. VAN VORST.

The life and character of Hamilton W. Robinson, in whose memory the bar of New York is this day assembled, are interesting to contemplate and study.

There was a remarkable unity in the development of his life from its beginning to its close.

In college, although among if not the youngest of his class, his whole course was marked by a diligent and thoughtful attention to his studies and duties.

He properly, although then a mere youth, regarded this period of his life as truly formative, and as likely to give direction and character to his future career. Evil habits were avoided and good ones formed.

I have heard him in after years speak with much feeling of the preparatory training and discipline which he received from his father, whose heart seemed wrapped up in the life and future of his son.

He gratefully acknowledged the ever present and inspiring influence that his father exercised on him.

He had marked out for himself a life of devotion to the profession of the law, in the principles of which he was always deeply interested. He always loved his profession, and in his life honored it.

His early training had prepared him for a useful and successful career. But this he knew could only be realized by constant study and earnest application.

He never suffered himself to be drawn aside from his duties, or to miss the mark upon which his eyes were always fixed, by any pursuits or interests which would hinder his onward progress.

As his tastes would have preferred, so he was led into a plane of professional business important in its character, and which gave full play to the excellent qualities of his mind. The interests of his litigations were generally large, and the legal questions involved serious.

While a junior to others, much of the effective preparation of cases fell upon him. He seemed to anticipate and guard himself and his case against all difficulties likely to arise, and was prepared to meet unusual exigencies. He enjoyed the confidence of his clients to a large degree. This confidence was always merited and respected, and to the end of his life he held the esteem of all with whom he had held professional relations.

He was fitted by education, training, and mental constitution to be a Judge.

And in the course of years, he was called to a place upon the bench of this honorable Court. But on the day he took his seat with his respected associates, he was in truth already an experienced and useful Judge.

He had been disciplined into habits of careful thought and sound judgment.

He was already fitted thoroughly to analyze evidence, and reach the truth amid conflicting statements, and to apply the controlling legal principles. He had an inborn love of justice and equity. He was always considerate and impartial. He was not hasty in his conclusions, but accepted results only when his judgment and conscience were satisfied. He had a just regard for authority, which he had been educated to respect, and in decisions always remembered that it was the province of the Judge to interpret and not to make the law.

When his judgments and decisions come to be considered, they will be found to be reasonable and just in their scope and substance, and clear and logical in statement. He was patient in the hearing of causes, kind, considerate and courteous in his demeanor to counsel engaged. The cause of justice and the rights of parties were always safe in his hands. And although his life, measured by years, was not long, yet through its work and fruit it was complete and beautifully rounded.

"That life is long which answers life's great end," and in this regard his work was thoroughly well done.

We may well deplore the loss of one so excellent as a man, so sincere and kind as a friend, and so upright and just as a judge.

ADDRESS OF CHIEF JUSTICE CHARLES P. DALY.

It is proper, gentlemen, that some expression should be given by this Court, of which Judge Robinson was a member, on the loss it has sustained in his decease. It is very gratifying to us, his late colleagues, to hear the tribute paid to his memory in the remarks which have just been made, and to witness the even much more substantial tribute paid by this large assemblage of the profession. It was at my particular request that Judge Robinson consented to become a candidate for the judgeship of this Court. We had reason to be particularly gratified, as he had previously declined a nomination for Judge of the Court of Appeals, and at a period when his election to that position was deemed certain; an assurance which was confirmed by the very large majority accorded to those who were afterwards elected. I say we had reason to be particularly gratified as members of the Court that he consented to become a candidate for election, and were much more so with the association that followed upon his election. I have had some experience in judicial life; I have had some contact with Judges, and a large contact with members of the bar, and I only pay a just tribute to my deceased colleague when I say that no one with whom I have ever come in contact in the discharge of intellectual duties, fulfiled, in my judgment, all the requirements so much as he did. Gentle in his nature, painstaking, accurate and conscientious, there was no amount of labor that he was not willing to bestow, no attention that he was not prepared to give. Where industry is stimulated by exceeding conscientiousness as it was in his case, it naturally followed that great confidence was felt in his conclusions, springing as they did from so pure a motive, and after so diligent and laborious an exercise of all the qualities which are requisite to secure a sound judgment upon anything. It was not only in this respect that he was most valuable to us, but if I may be permitted to say what is not common upon public occasions, he was very dear to us for other qualities. I think there is an old Russian proverb that says, "You never know anything of a man until you have made a campaign with him;" and my experience is that you know comparatively little of a Judge unless you are associated with him in the discharge of official duties. You then see more clearly the motives by which he is actuated. You see a great deal which the world can never see. You get an insight into his finer and better qualities which is not perceptible to those outside; and it is this knowledge which makes the loss of Judge Robinson to us a very great one. We can all unite in the statement that during the period he was in the Court the greatest harmony prevailed in our intercourse with him, which was never in any way affected. When there was difference of judgment on his part there was always that kindly bearing which it is easy to remember, but difficult to express; a uniformity and gentleness of character which was exceedingly attractive in official intercourse. He always met us with a pleasant smile, and such a thing as an unkindly word never passed his lips; nor so far as the human countenance is an index did he ever appear to harbor an unkindly thought. We are especially grateful to the gentlemen who have taken the trouble upon this occasion to call particular attention to the special merits of our deceased colleague—Mr. Marsh, Judge Birdseye and Judge Van Vorst. They have dwelt upon the intellectual and moral qualities by which he was distinguished so fully that it is unnecessary for me to say anything more. I can only say, gentlemen, in conclusion, that we feel his loss much more deeply than it is in our power to express, for those things are felt most which are beyond expression. We are exceedingly grateful for the tribute which has been paid to his memory, and none know better than we do how justly it has been bestowed.

The question was then put upon the adoption of the resolution that had been offered by Mr. Vanderpoel, and the resolutions were adopted.

Upon motion of Mr. Charles Tracy, the secretary of the meeting was directed to transmit a copy of the resolutions to the family of Judge Robinson, and also to furnish copies to the public press for publication.

The meeting then adjourned.

After the death of Judge Hamilton W. Robinson, who was succeeded by Judge Miles Beach, Judge Charles H. Van Brunt was elected to the Supreme Court in 1883, his successor being Judge Henry Wilder Allen. Judges Joseph F. Daly, Richard L. Larremore and Henry Wilder Allen had been re-elected for full terms in 1874. The next meeting of the bar, in the rooms of the Court of Common Pleas, was convened on the occasion of the retirement of Chief Justice Charles P. Daly, whose term of office expired December 31, 1885, and who was ineligible to re-election by reason of the constitutional limit as to age. This interesting event was the occasion of an immense gathering of members of the bar in the General Term room. The proceedings are reported in full on the next page and the general expression of public opinion on the incident, as voiced by the press, will be found in the appendix.

PROCEEDINGS OF THE BAR OF THE CITY OF NEW YORK ON THE RETIREMENT OF CHIEF JUSTICE CHARLES. P. DALY.

A meeting of the bar was held December 30th, 1885, in the General Term room of the Court of Common Pleas at 3 P.M., for the purpose of uniting in an expression of respect for the character and services of Chief Justice Daly, on his retirement from the bench. The signers to the call for this meeting were: David Dudley Field, Wm. Allen Butler, Aaron J. Vanderpoel, Charles A. Peabody, Clarence A. Seward, F. R. Coudert, John M. Scribner, Isaac P. Martin, J. E. Burrill, Aaron P. Whitehead, M. W. Divine, James C. Carter, Luther R. Marsh, John L. Cadwalader. Wm. D. Shipman, Wm. G. Choate, Edw'd Patterson, George Zabriskie, Osborn E. Bright, Grosvenor Lowrey, Chas. M. Da Costa, Ch. Francis Stone, C. W. Bangs, Algernon S. Sullivan, Almon Goodwin, E. R. Robinson, Theron G. Strong, Elihu Root, Fordham Morris, Joseph H. Choate, Charles C. Beaman, George C. Holt, Francis Lynde Stetson, John W. Sterling, Duncan Smith, E. B. Hinsdale, Edward D. Sprague, Austen G Fox, Cephas Brainerd, Henry H. Anderson, F. F. Marbury, W. M. Prichard.

Ex-President Chester A. Arthur presided, and on either side of him were the vice-presidents, ex-Judge

Henry Hilton, Justices Van Brunt, Barrett, Brady and Van Vorst and ex-Judge Frederick W. Loew, all of whom have been Judges of the Court. Among those present, in addition to those who signed the call for the meeting were ex-Judge Edwards Pierrepont, ex-Governor John T. Hoffman, Henry L. Clinton, Abram Wakeman, Judge-elect Henry W. Bookstaver, Amasa A. Redfield, Frank Loomis, Rufus F. Andrews, Robert Sewell, ex-Judge A. J. Dittenhoefer, John O. Mott, Peter B. Olney, Frederick G. Gedney, Douglas Taylor, Rastus B. Ransom, John Sherwood, ex-Judge William H. Arnoux, Anthony M. Keiley and many others. Sitting with the Judges within the rail was Chief Justice Daly, the observed of all observers. He listened with heightened color to the warm encomiums passed upon him, but when he rose to reply he was as calm in manner and self-possessed as if dealing with an ordinary motion. Ex-President Arthur took the chair at the nomination of Algernon S. Sullivan.

ADDRESS OF EX-PRESIDENT ARTHUR.

GENTLEMEN OF THE BAR:—It is with no slight reluctance that I accept the office to which your generous preference has called me, for I cannot forget that these many years I have been a "truant in the law," and that at no time have I been worthy to be classed among its conspicuous practitioners. We have gathered here to pay our glad tribute of affection and respect to one who more than two score years ago,

> "His years but young, but his experience old,
> His head unmellowed, but his judgment ripe,"

was called to the bench of our Court of Common Pleas. How admirably he has ever since discharged the duties upon which he then entered, this company of lawyers know, and some among you will to-day bear witness. Their province I shall not usurp. It is for them, and not for me, to dwell upon that love of truth and justice, that courtesy and candor, that wide and profound learning, that strict impartiality and stainless integrity which have ever distinguished Judge Daly's juridical life, and because of which his retirement from the bench cannot fail to be attended with deep and general regret. To whom else, indeed, could be more fittingly applied the encomium of Richard Baxter upon Sir Matthew Hale: "That pattern of Judges, entering upon, using and voluntarily surrounding his place of judicature with the most universal love, honor and praise?" Gentlemen, what is your pleasure?

ADDRESS OF MR. DAVID DUDLEY FIELD.

Mr. Chairman and Gentlemen:—When we see a man of three score years and ten wearing his faculties unimpaired, dwelling with satisfaction upon the past, enjoying the present, and looking cheerfully into the future, we congratulate him upon his serene old age. And if he has been as mindful of his public as of his private duties, helping to form and reform parties, to make and unmake magistrates, and to shape the policy and the fate of that wondrous organism, the body politic, we call him a deserving citizen. If he has borne public office to public satisfaction, we commend him for the honorable performance of his duty to the commonwealth. And if the office has been judicial, and he has borne it long, and borne it well, so well, indeed, that no one blames, but all men praise him, we pronounce him thrice happy.

These conditions are fulfiled in the friend whom we are here to receive and greet on his descent from the bench. He has lived a manly and blameless life; he has been a faithful citizen of the dual republic into which he was born, that lesser republic the State, and that greater the Nation, to which the State belongs, and he has discharged the functions of high judicial magistracy for nearly half a century, without fear and without reproach.

This is not the place nor the occasion for eulogy, which would be as unpleasant for him to hear as it would be unbecoming in me to speak, but the most fastidious taste would not refuse me the privilege of saying that there must be something remarkable in one who has had the rare distinction of having been once appointed by the Executive and five times chosen by universal suffrage to the same high judicial office, who has walked unharmed over the hot plowshares of popular elections, and filled his station for nearly two-and-forty years, twenty-seven of them as the Chief Justice, to the general acceptance of all our citizens. Some details of his life are to be mentioned by the gentleman who will follow me. I will say no more than that he had the great advantage of beginning without patrimony, actual or expectant. He started in the race of life, free of the impediment which hinders so many of our youth; but he had a stout heart and a steady hand, and with these he went forth into the world. His first venture was on the sea, where he acquired that taste for travel and love of geography which have distinguished him since. In one of his voyages it was his good fortune to see the capture of Algiers by the French. Who of us would not have toiled hard to see the lifting of that curtain which had hung so long over the southern shores of the Mediterranean, and the opening of a new drama on the theatre of the Dark Continent? Returning from the sea to the land, he threw in his lot with the great and honorable company of mechanics, until the advice of a friend led him away to the law, where, as we all know, he has been an apt scholar and a great teacher.

Consider for a moment the nature of the judicial office. The judgment seat has been accorded in history sacred and profane the chief place of honor. The praise of the greatest of men was that he sat in the " seat of judgment." If this was so in former days, how much higher has the seat been raised in our day and country. The ever-enlarging circle of civilization, the development of industrial arts, the strides of commerce, the accumulation of corporate wealth; and above all the subordination of the law-giver to a written constitution, as the supreme will of the sovereign people, all these have invested the office of Judge with a dignity and power the past never knew. What new responsibility do they not entail! What qualities of intellect and will, what laborious study, what patient forbearance, what self-control do they not require; and I will add, what increase of danger do they not bring!

I appeal, then, to all who hear me, whether our friend has not earned that good name, that affluence of respect, which by common consent he bears. He has held office by choice of the executive and votes of the people. He has lived under the old dispensation and the new. His half-century of service is a long link in that endless chain of law, which began with society and will end only when society is dissolved. With what unswerving honesty, what quiet dignity, what honorable simplicity, he has discharged his great trust, we, who are his witnesses, can testify. Who has seen him indifferent to the duties of his place? None. Who has seen him turn to the right hand or the left for any man's frown or any man's favor? None. Who has heard him discuss out of Court what was to be decided in Court? Nobody. Who has believed him to be moved in his judgments by any consideration but the law and the testimony? Not one. Let us then greet him as victor, coming to us from the arena; one who has honored himself and in doing that has honored us.

Mr. Field concluded by offering the following resolution for the consideration of the meeting:

RESOLUTION.

The retirement of Chief Justice Charles P. Daly from the bench of the Common Pleas, where he has served for more than forty-one years, and presided for twenty-seven, appears to us, members of the bar of the City and County of New York, a fitting occasion for expressing our respect for his private character and our commendation of his judicial career. To have passed safely for more than two score years through the trials of judicial life, encountering meantime the ordeal of

Theodore W. Dwight.

Austin Abbott.

JAMES C. CARTER.

BENJAMIN F. TRACY.

five popular elections, and leaving in the minds of all citizens the conviction that he has always administered justice without fear or favor, caring only for the law and the testimony, which he diligently studied—these things, combining with the uniform courtesy, patience and impartiality which have characterized his entire course with the bar, have given him a place pre-eminent in our regards, and lead us to salute him with our most respectful homage, as he descends from the bench of this tribunal. And while we give him this salutation for the past, we wish him for the future long life and that happiness in rest from judicial labor which springs from one's own self-respect, and a life well spent in the service of God and his fellow-men.

ADDRESS OF MR. WILLIAM ALLEN BUTLER.

Mr. Chairman: The privilege is accorded to me of seconding the resolutions just offered, which I am sure express the unanimous sentiments of the bar of this city on this occasion, marked by so much of peculiar interest and significance.

However we may differ in individual opinion as to the wisdom of that provision of Section 13 of the Sixth Article of the Constitution of this State which cuts the thread of the judicial tenure at the age of three score years and ten, we are grateful for the opportunity it gives us to-day of testifying our respect and regard for the retiring Chief Justice of this honorable Court, who, having helped, as a member of the Constitutional Convention, to frame this very section, now feels its force; as the struck eagle of the poet's fancy

"Viewed his own feather in the fatal dart,
And winged the shaft that quivers in his heart."

We are all reluctant to concede the facts which require the application of the constitutional mandate to Chief Justice Daly. Could our suffrages prevail, we would gladly imitate the example set, day before yesterday, by the great Republic of France in continuing in its highest office one whose years number seventy-three.* But we have no alternative. Against the presumption of fitness arising from our observation of his unimpaired mental and physical vigor, we are met by his candid admission and by the conclusive evidence on the files of this Court, and so by force of a kind of inequitable estoppel, both *in pais* and by the record, the organic law, not of nature, but of the State, adjudges his retirement.

When this Court was organized by the Act of 1821, the tenure of office of its Judges was during good behavior, or until the age of sixty years was attained. This provision was similar to that of the Constitution of 1821, following the earlier Constitution, and it applied to the Chancellor and the Justices of the Supreme Court. Our present Constitution has lengthened the span of the judicial life by a decade, and the judiciary itself has improved on the Constitution by the repeated instances it has afforded of unimpaired faculties and fitness in incumbents of the bench when the limit of their terms had been reached. As it was with

---

* This happy reference of Mr. Butler's was to the re-election of President Grévy, whose term as President of the French Republic was expiring, and who was re-elected to his high office at the age of seventy-three, in December, 1885, just before the retirement of Chief Justice Daly.

them, so it is with our retiring Chief Justice; the shadow crosses the dial and marks the appointed hour; the object on which it falls still stands erect and in the sunlight.

The resolutions fitly emphasize the long duration of his term of office now about to expire; a term longer by ten years than the judicial life of Lord Mansfield, and by nearly ten years that of Judge Story. The illustrious career of Judge Samuel Nelson, reaching to within a few months of a full half century of judicial service, embraced his term in the Supreme Court of the United States as well as that in the Supreme Court of this State. The peculiar feature of the judicial life of Chief Justice Daly is that it has been spent in this single sphere of duty, within the limits of this city, and the precincts of this Court. To have served as Associate Judge, First Judge and Chief Justice of the Court of Common Pleas for the City and County of New York is to have held a foremost place as a judicial officer in the commercial centre of the nation, during the most eventful period in the history of our jurisprudence; a period marked by progress and reform; by the simplification of the methods of procedure; by the application of the principles of justice to all the new and unprecedented activities of the age; by the enlargement of the field of judicial cognizance and research through the aid of science and the inexhaustible energies of commerce; by the investiture of the Courts of Common Law with the benignant powers of equitable jurisdiction; and by the unexampled advance of freedom and the rights of man.

This growth and advance are well illustrated in the

history of this tribunal, and in the experience of its Chief Justice. At first, an outgrowth of the Mayor's Court—a purely municipal organization—it was committed in 1821 to the care of a single Judge. Afterwards, as the city grew and its commerce was enlarged, the number of its Judges was, from time to time, increased, and the jurisdiction of the Court extended, until now, with its common law and equity jurisdiction it is, substantially, coördinate with the Supreme Court. I cannot but think that the Chief Justice must have exerted some occult influence over the Reformers of 1848, when the whole nomenclature of pleading was swept away, and pleas in abatement, pleas *puis darrein*, rejoinders, rebutters, and surrebutters, went by the board. Nothing was saved except the demurrer—which no honest defendant will ever part with—and the name of this Court, which remains unchanged. It is a link between the judicial system of to-day and that which was administered by the Court, when, in 1844, Chief Justice Daly first took the oath of office and found himself encircled, but not entangled, by the network of special pleas woven by such veteran experts of the common law as John Anthon, James W. Gerard, Charles O'Conor, Daniel Lord and their many compeers, whom time fails me to mention, but whose names your memories will supply.

Very near to the people in its original and its appellate jurisdiction, this Court has commanded the respect of the bench and the bar, by the character of its Judges, and the weight of their decisions, a respect largely due, as many of us can testify, to the personal probity, the undeviating courtesy, the ability, the

Clarence A. Seward

Joseph H. Choate

Elihu Root

John S. McCook

industry and painstaking of the learned and accomplished jurist who for more than two score years has aided in its administration of justice, and for more than a quarter of a century has been its Presiding Judge. Standing thus as a representative of the past as well as the present judicial system, we may well point to the Chief Justice as an example of the best working of both; and as illustrating, in his person and career, the excellence of the Judges we had when Judges were appointed, and the excellence of the Judges we have had since Judges became elective; while his protracted term certainly vindicates the wisdom of the popular suffrage by which his long continuance in office has been secured.

I can only advert, in passing, to special instances of decisions and opinions, in conspicuous cases, which will remain as permanent memorials of the legal ability and skill of Chief Justice Daly, and to his varied and versatile labors in the field of literature, and to his intelligent and long-continued work in the department of geographical exploration and research. The admiration and encomium of Baron Von Humboldt, as expressed in his published letters, in regard to the learning and accomplishments of the Chief Justice, are a just tribute, the truthfulness of which will be attested by many voices at home and in Europe. As President of the Geographical Society we congratulate him on retaining a jurisdiction co-extensive with the great globe itself.

I cannot close without adverting to another characteristic of the Chief Justice—his sterling integrity. This, it may be said, is superfluous. Integrity is a primal and necessary element of the judicial character, without whose authenticating stamp it would be a base or a counterfeit thing. But, as in the solar spectrum, while the prismatic colors are always the same, their brightness is enhanced according to the purity of the medium through which they pass, so when the honesty of the Judge is the exhibition of the purity of the individual character, we may well accord it the meed of personal praise.

If our retrospect of the period covered by this long term of judicial service took in nothing at variance with the absolute integrity of the judicial character we might leave to silence this conspicuous trait. But we are only dealing truthfully with ourselves and with the great interests which, by virtue of our profession, we hold in trust, when we acknowledge our obligations to men who adorn and elevate the judicial function by stern, inflexible uprightness. It is because we have had, during that period, in this great city, in the midst of its greed, its temptations and its selfish competitions, on the bench of this Court, and of the other Courts within these walls, men of the stamp of Charles P. Daly, that the administration of justice remains to us, to-day, a safe and sacred thing; men of whom, as individuals, if judicial defection, as a strange, anomalous exception to the rule of judicial integrity, is ever abroad—worse than the pestilence that walketh in darkness, or the destruction that wasteth at noonday—we can truly say "It shall not come nigh thee." And it is a source of the highest satisfaction to us to-day to see the ideal of this high, unswerving judicial uprightness exemplified by a career such as that we now contemplate, which alike at its setting as at its dawn and its meridian has satisfied this first and supreme requirement.

Our citizens cannot too often be reminded that the main source of security and strength for our free institutions is in the due administration of justice, and nowhere is there greater need than here in this city that we properly understand and appreciate the absolute necessity of placing and keeping on the bench honest, capable and courageous men. The recent election marked the ascendency of sound views in this direction in the expression of the popular will in the reëlection of faithful Judges whose terms had expired, and but for the constitutional bar there would have been a unanimous reëlection of the Chief Justice whom, without undue adulation, but with honest praise, we honor to-day in this city of his birth and of his life-long labors, in the Court in which he has been a familiar presence for so many years, beside his co-workers of the bench with whom he has shared his responsibilities of faithful judicial service, and among his brethren of the bar who pay this united tribute, not only to the learned and upright Judge, but also to the true-hearted and large-hearted man.

Happy, says the Roman poet, is he to whom it is given to say, at each day's close: "I have lived."

" Laetus * * cui licet in diem
        Dixisse Vixi."

Certainly he is more to be felicitated who, in the evening of life, can look back over a career of public service begun in early manhood and pursued to the

171

final limit of permitted judicial labor, and say with truth that he has filled up the measure of usefulness and duty. Such satisfaction attends our venerated friend and brother, Chief Justice Daly, and as he quits his place of dignity and authority on this bench and lays aside the ermine, worn so worthily, he will be invested with the affection, esteem and best wishes of all his professional brethren on the bench and at the bar, and with the grateful respect of the community he has served so long and so well.

ADDRESS OF JUDGE RICHARD O'GORMAN.

Judge O'Gorman said that no word of his could heighten the interest of this occasion, which had brought together so many distinguished members of the bar. They felt the joy of the friend, the pride of the fellow-lawyer and citizen that one of them should have deserved so great praise as was awarded to Chief Justice Daly. The only regret was that the public was to lose the services of an officer still in the prime of intellectual vigor. The occasion was one almost unprecedented. For forty-one years Charles P. Daly had been a Judge of the Court of Common Pleas and for twenty-seven years Chief Justice. The office was full of care and responsibility and he had filled it in the full glare of publicity for all these years. He had played his great judicial part, and, like the actor turning to leave the stage, awaited the verdict, which was unanimously in his favor. The presiding officer of this meeting had lately laid down his office as the head of the Goverment with unostentatious dignity, carrying with him golden opinions from all, and this vast meeting of prominent members of the

172

Wm. H. Hubbard

Thomas G. Shearman

Julien T. Davies

Wager Swayne

bar, presided over by him, was not one of unmeaning flattery of the retiring jurist. His impartiality, his suavity and fair treatment of all had made him friends among all parties.

Judge O'Gorman's speech was very earnest and eloquent.

ADDRESS OF JUDGE RICHARD L. LARREMORE.

The Court of which Chief Justice Daly is the retiring member asks the privilege of adding another leaf to the closing chapter of his judicial life. His associates wholly appreciate the delicate but still deserved compliment which the occasion commemorates. We feel honored and encouraged by this public recognition of a long and useful judicial career. Over fifteen years of personal and professional intercourse have taught us the value of Charles P. Daly to the Court of Common Pleas. He has been so long and closely identified with it that it may be said without affectation or extravagance he represented it. Born in the old school of our profession, he has never forgotten his early training in exhaustive and elaborate investigation; yet has he always been keenly alive to that progressive spirit which would simplify the practice and enlarge the benefits of the law which he administered. Of his ability and success as a jurist it is unnecessary to speak. His decisions form no inconspicuous part of the jurisprudence of the State, and may safely be left to stand upon their own merits. In his social and judicial relations he has always been the dignified gentleman and jurist. Kindness and courtesy have always characterized his action. This has been continuously manifested, not only to his immediate associates, but to all who came within the contact of his influence. It has so happened that in small matters our honored Chief Justice has won our admiration and respect. Whether the amount in litigation was $2 or $200,000, the same patient care and scrutiny were always exercised. Faithful in the least, he has necessarily been faithful in much; and none except those immediately interested will ever know how firmly he has always withstood the encroachments of the powerful upon the rights of the lowly. Apart from his judicial life, Charles P. Daly is favorably known and recognized in the departments of literature and science. We are greatly gratified that from the onerous requirements of his strict professional calling he has found time and opportunity (without neglect of official duties) to diverge his attention and influence in other channels of usefulness. Our most intimate relations with him have been as colleagues of an upright, capable, conscientious Judge, whose judicial career for over forty-one years will ever inspire our zeal and invest his memory with many cherished associations. Nothing more remains to be said. It is a comfort to feel that we have not met under the shadow of a death, but in the ripened life of a living jurist who is permitted to know and realize his exact place in public estimation. The Court of Common Pleas, Mr. President, gratefully acknowledges this expression of the interest by yourself and the assembly in the career of Chief Justice Daly, and unites in the anticipation that his future life will find repose in contemplation of

"Duty well done and joy well earned."

It is a very inadequate expression of my feelings to say that I am deeply moved by this demonstration, not only from what has been said, but by this large assemblage of the bar and by the honor you have done me, sir [turning to the ex-President], by presiding on this occasion. It is embarrassing under any circumstances to listen to one's own commendation, and more embarrassing still to reply to it. When I went upon the bench at the early age of twenty-eight, it was not without a sense of the importance of the judicial office and of how little I was qualified to fill it, from my youth, my limited learning and want of experience; for which I had at least this excuse, that I had not been an applicant for the office; that I declined the appointment when it was first offered to me, and accepted it finally only upon the advice of Governor Marcy, as the consummation of an arrangement that satisfied others who had been contestants for the place. Accepting it under such circumstances, I resolved earnestly to endeavor to do my duty, and now that I am about to withdraw from it after an official service of more than ordinary duration, it is very gratifying to receive this public acknowledgment that you think that I have done so. It is gratifying for several reasons. Erasmus has prefigured the general situation of a Judge in the exclamation of "Unhappy is the man who sees both sides," to which may be added, and still more unhappy is he who hopes to satisfy both sides. I early recognized this truth, and when I had applied all my powers to the examination of a case, and had decided it, I never thought of it afterwards; and as a Judge's duties lie chiefly in the settlement of legal controversies in which one party is gratified and the other disappointed, it is very satisfactory for me to feel that, as far as I know, the discharge of this duty over so many years has left behind it no unpleasant recollections.

There is another reason why this demonstration is gratifying. I made it a rule very early in my career, from an experience which I had had, that I never would reply to or seek to correct any misrepresentation or erroneous statement respecting myself in public journals, of which, during my long career, I have had my share—that I would leave everything of this kind to time. This was sometimes hard to bear. During the rule of what was known as the "Ring," in this city, my name was made use of and appeared in the public journals without my knowledge, authority or approval as one of a board of trustees for the receipt of money for the erection of a statue in this city to William M. Tweed. It was very hard in this case to adhere to that resolution; but I did, and this meeting is, at least to me, an assurance that I lost nothing by doing so.

In receiving this acknowledgment on the part of the members of the bar, I have also to make my acknowledgements to them; for I can say, as Lord Mansfield said upon a like occasion, if I have given satisfaction it is owing to the learning and assistance of the bar. It is due to them also to say that I have, especially in my later years, been the recipient of great courtesy at their hands; that the instances, if any, have been few in which I have experienced any rudeness or discourtesy from any member of the profession. I feel this the more because judges, in the discharge of their duties, cannot always be as affable or as courteous as they would be under other circumstances. Having generally to give the closest attention to the matter before them—to concentrate all their faculties for the immediate decision of questions that may be new, intricate or difficult—the earnest discharge of such duties frequently brings about a highly nervous condition that shows itself in a brusqueness of manner and curtness of speech that sometimes gives offense when none was intended, and as I have, with my judicial brethren, shared in this infirmity, I feel, as I have said, more sensibly, the courtesy always shown me by the bar.

As I look around among the faces of the members of it present I see from the appearance of some of them that they could not have been born when I went upon the bench. This reminds me more than the enumeration of years, of the length of time I have passed in the discharge of judicial duties, and recalls also how many, during that time, have passed away, with whose faces and whose voices I was so long familiar. This is not the occasion, however, to indulge in a retrospect of the past. At some future time I hope to call attention to many of my distinguished contemporaries by embodying in some permanent shape, as I have frequently been asked to do, my recollections of the bench and the bar of this city during the past fifty years.

In conclusion, allow me to say, gentlemen, that though leaving the bench, I do not intend to separate myself entirely from the profession. Accustomed as I have been for the past forty-one years to go down town every morning to business, I do not deem it wise to give up that habit as long as my mental and bodily faculties remain unimpaired. A long experience has taught me that the happiest life is a life of labor when it is properly intermingled with rest, recreation and exercise, and as I propose to continue it in the pursuits of the profession hereafter, I trust that my relations with my legal brethren in the future will continue to be as pleasant as they have been in the past.

PRESENTATION OF A GAVEL TO CHIEF JUSTICE CHARLES P. DALY.

Nathaniel Jarvis, Jr., Clerk of the Court of Common Pleas, then stepped forward and placed in the hands of the presiding officer the gavel wielded by Chief Justice Daly for so many years, and requested him to present it to the retiring jurist. Ex-President Arthur placed it in the hands of Justice Daly and said:

Chief Justice, it gives me great pleasure to present to you, on behalf of the Clerks of the Court of Common Pleas, the gavel that you have wielded so many years with so much honor and dignity.

This was received with a bow, and the meeting was adjourned.

INSCRIPTION UPON THE GAVEL.

Both heads of the gavel are encased in gold. On one head is the arms of the City combined with those of the State. Above the arms is the name CHARLES P. DALY, and below the motto *Suscipere et Finire* (to undertake and complete), and on either side of the arms are the dates 1844–1885. On the gold plate of the other head is this inscription:

This gavel was used by
MICHAEL ULSHOEFFER, First Judge,
From 1838 to 1850.

DANIEL INGRAHAM, First Judge,
From 1850 to 1857.

CHARLES P. DALY, First Judge,
From 1857 to 1871.

CHARLES P. DALY, Chief Justice,
From 1871 to 1885.

Upon the shank of the handle, which is surrounded by
a gold plate, is the passage from Shakespeare's "Merchant of Venice,"

"———— O wise and upright judge,
How much more elder art thou than thy looks?"

The gavel was contained in an oaken box, highly
polished, having a gold plate on the lid with the inscription:

CHAS. P. DALY,
HÆC OLIM MEMINISSE JUVABIT,
1885.

which may be rendered, "Hereafter it may be pleasant
to recall these things."

PRESENTATION OF A MEMORIAL TABLET OF JUDGE HAMILTON W. ROBINSON, ON DECEMBER 2, 1895.

There was a crowded attendance in the General Term room of the Court of Common Pleas on Monday, December 2d, 1895, to witness the presentation to the Court by the bar of New York, of the bronze memorial tablet in honor of Judge Hamilton W. Robinson. The tablet occupies a position immediately under the oil painting of Judge Robinson.

The tablet was presented in brief addresses by former Chief Justice Charles P. Daly and John E. Parsons.

ADDRESS OF EX-CHIEF JUSTICE CHARLES P. DALY.

I rise to offer and ask the acceptance of this cenotaph or tablet as a memorial of Hamilton W. Robinson. This Court, after an existence of two hundred and forty-two years, passes away at the end of this month, and it is our wish while it is still in being to place upon the wall of the chamber where it is now sitting this cenotaph in memory of one of its most satisfactory Judges. I say satisfactory, for we do not claim for Judge Robinson the distinction expressed by the words "a great judge." Horace Binney, in his eulogy of Chief Justice Marshall, said that the world had produced fewer great Judges than it has of great men in any other department of civil life. In

IN·MEMORY·OF
HAMILTON·W·ROBINSON

BORN·NOV·25·1814   DIED·APRIL·7·1879

JUDGE·OF·THE·COURT·OF·COMMON·PLEAS·FOR
THE·CITY·AND·COUNTY·OF·NEW·YORK·1870·1879
AN·HONOR·TO·THE·JUDICIARY·AND·TO·OUR·PROFESSION

HIS·URBANITY·AND·SINCERITY·ENDEARED·HIM·TO·US·AND·HIS·PROBITY
HIS·LEARNING·AND·HIS·FAITHFULNESS·TO·DUTY·COMMANDED
UNIVERSAL·RESPECT·WE·CHERISH·PLEASANT·RECOLLECTIONS·OF

HIS·WELL·SPENT·LIFE·AND·REVERE·HIS·MEMORY·AS
AN·ABLE·AND·UPRIGHT·JUDGE

RESOLUTIONS·OF·BENCH·AND·BAR   APRIL·24·1879

confirmation of this I may add that when a few months ago I visited Westminster Abbey, the mausoleum of England's distinguished dead, in going over that grand home of departed statesmen, commanders, historians and theologians, I found but four memorials to Judges, and only one of them, Lord Mansfield, could be called a great Judge.   Of the other three, only Sir Robert Atkyn, Chief Baron of the Exchequer in the time of William III., was a man of pre-eminent attainments; and of the others, Sir Thomas Bramwell, who presided at the trial of Mary Queen of Scots, and Sir Thomas Richardson, once Chief Justice, it may be said that they received the distinction of a memorial in Westminster Abbey for some other cause than their learning and ability as Judges.   Burke has said that the intelligent administration of law is the cement of human society, and upon it we depend for the preservation of life, liberty and property.   For this we rely on those who fill judicial office.   To fill this high trust, it is not necessary that he who fills it should be a great Judge. That distinction is due to times and circumstances as much as to ability.

All who knew Judge Robinson judicially knew he was a model Judge in the important qualities of industry in acquiring knowledge of the law, and discrimination in applying it, in uprightness, in patience, and in the thorough investigation of cases decided by him.   No Judge of the Court ever followed more fully the spirit of the prayer for divine guidance used at the first session of the Court on February 2d, 1653.   It is a benefit to society to make permanent record of such a judicial example.   The sentiment that prompts it is an old one.

Archæologists dig up in Egypt and on the banks of the
Tigris and Euphrates memorials of those past civic
fraternities that indicate how deep seated is the disposition to honor departed worth.

This occasion recalls the meeting held over sixteen
years ago in this room, when the leaders of the bar and
Judges representing all the Courts, Federal and State,
of this district met to testify their sorrow at the death
of Judge Robinson, their esteem and affection for him
as a man and their respect for the commanding position
in the judiciary and the profession which his ability and
industry had gained for him.   You, Judge Daly, then
the Chief Justice of this Court, of which Judge Robinson was a member, were unanimously elected to preside
over the meeting.   The vice-presidents included the
then five Justices of the Supreme Court, of whom only
two are now on the bench; the six Justices of the
Superior Court, of whom two only now survive; Judge
Blatchford, then United States Circuit Judge, who has
followed into rest so many of his judicial contemporaries; Judge William G. Choate, then United States
District Judge, and five eminent lawyers now no more
—Charles O'Conor, David Dudley Field, John K. Porter, William A. Beach, and Stephen D. Law.   Among
the secretaries was John M. Scribner, who commenced
his professional career as an associate of Judge Robinson before he ascended the bench, and who is present
with us to-day.

On that day, April 24th, 1879, addresses were deliv-

182

ered by the favorite of the bar, Aaron J. Vanderpoel, by Judge Lucien Birdseye, Mr. Luther R. Marsh, Judge Van Vorst, and by Chief Justice Charles P. Daly.

Never was there a meeting of the bar which had less of mere formality and more of genuine personal feeling. Judge Robinson had been taken away by death in the fulness of his powers, in the prime of life, in the midst of his active judicial labors, while the witnesses of his early efforts still survived, and there was not an expression of regret uttered that day which did not come from a full heart and reach a responsive listener.

The lapse of sixteen years finds his memory still cherished by the members of the bar. One of his then associates on the bench, distinguished for the soundness and vigor of his judicial opinions, has taken the leading part in the preparation of the beautiful and fitting tablet which is to-day unveiled in its place in these halls. With Judge Van Hoesen comes also the former Chief Justice of the Court, who, ten years after laying down the cares of office, in obedience to the constitutional mandate which fixes the limit of judicial service, appears full of strength and power, which we all hope and trust may be continued him for many years to come.

Judge Robinson deserves these tributes as a man. The years which I spent with him in the closest friendship and united by the strongest ties showed me that he possessed a heart full of good will, generosity, forbearance, patience and love. His disposition was transparently candid and open; no corner of it harbored an inclination to injure a fellow-man for any cause or upon

183

any provocation. He was possessed of the tenderest feelings; a slight to one of his friends wounded him more deeply and lastingly than the person for whom it was intended; an affront to himself, though keenly felt, was pardoned and forgotten.

A great lawyer among the greatest lawyers of his time, a loved companion of the brightest wits of the bar, the kindest, gentlest and most considerate of associates, his union of gifts and qualities showed a fine blending of the natural and spiritual in his life. I will not lift the curtain from the sanctity of his inner life more than is sufficient to disclose to the generation that succeeds him that he was unaffectedly and sincerely reverent—a quality indispensable to true greatness of purpose and achievement. In one sense only was he a public man, and that was in the exercise of his judicial functions. In politics as such his busy professional career left him no time to mix; but he was personally known to men who in his time swayed the political destiny of the State, and there was not one of them who did not love and respect his uprightness, independence and high sense of duty. As we see to-day, the recollection of these qualities time has not been able to efface nor length of years to deaden.

It is in memory then of one of our most eminent Judges, one of our dearest associates, one of our most exemplary citizens, that you present to the Court which he adorned the commemorative tablet now unveiled; and we accept it on behalf of our Court, of the whole judicial body of the county and of the whole community which witnessed and profited by his great judicial service.

DAVID MC CLURE.

WILLIAM B. HORNBLOWER.

WILLIAM ALLEN BUTLER.

JOHN H. V. ARNOLD.

MEETING OF THE BAR AT THE CLOSING OF THE EXISTENCE OF THE COURT OF COMMON PLEAS, DECEMBER 30, 1895.

Pursuant to the invitation of a Committee of Arrangements composed of Hon. George M. Van Hoesen, chairman; Austen G. Fox, James R. Cuming, John M. Scribner, William Hildreth Field, George L. Rives, Ferdinand Kurzman, David McClure and James P. Davenport, who were appointed at a preliminary meeting "to make arrangements for exercises that shall commemorate the respect and good feeling that the bar of New York has always entertained for the Court of Common Pleas," the members of the bar assembled in the General Term room of the Court in the County Court House, at 2 o'clock P. M., on Monday, December 30th, 1895, the day before the date fixed for the dissolution of the Court under the new Constitution consolidating all the Superior Courts of cities with the Supreme Court of the State.

There were present besides the Judges of the Court, Presiding Justice Van Brunt of the Supreme Court; the Judges of the Superior Court of the City of New York; the Surrogates; the Judges of the General Sessions; the Justices of the City Court of New York; the Justices of the District Courts; the former Judges of the Common Pleas, Charles P. Daly, Henry Hilton, and George M. Van Hoesen, the members of the committee, and a vast concourse of members of the bar which filled the room so completely that many were unable to gain admittance. Upon the entrance of the Judges from the private chambers they were received with great applause.

The meeting was called to order by ex-Judge Van Hoesen, who nominated for chairman Chief Justice Joseph F. Daly. The motion was seconded and carried unanimously and Charles A. Runk and John Proctor Clarke were named a committee to inform the Chief Justice that he had been selected to preside. As the Chief Justice entered and assumed his place he was received with prolonged applause. On nomination of ex-Judge Van Hoesen, Mr. Wilbur Larremore, son of former Chief Justice Richard L. Larremore; Mr. Henry A. Robinson, son of former Judge Hamilton W. Robinson, and Mr. George Irving, son of the First Judge John T. Irving, were requested to act as secretaries. The secretaries took positions on the bench with the Chief Justice and the other Judges present.

The Chairman desired to know the pleasure of the meeting, upon which Mr. David McClure rose and said:

ADDRESS OF MR. DAVID MC CLURE.

Mr. Chairman and Gentlemen:

This occasion impresses me as of more than passing interest, meriting all of the attention it has attracted.

When, in 1882, in London, the Courts of Law located in Westminister Hall, and the Courts of Chancery in Chancery Lane, were transferred to the new Royal Courts of Law, the occasion was deemed of sufficient importance to warrant ceremonies participated in by

England's Queen, Lord Chancellor and Lord Chief Justice before a gathering including that country's most distinguished citizens: this, although the occasion was simply the change of abode of the Courts in question. And those Courts were by those ceremonies dignified before the people of England, and that people's respect and reverence for them increased.

To us, this occasion is vastly more momentous. A Court with a past reaching back to the earliest days of our municipal, and far beyond our national, life, whose record is honorable and meritorious, is about, if not to die, to at least in the marriage of the Courts about to take place, lose that identity and name which it has held for more than two centuries.

It is therefore "good for us to be here?" It is proper that we should pause for a moment in these fleeting hours of a year fast passing away, a season significant of death and life, the old and the new, and while giving voice to the confident expectation that the consolidated Court of which the Judges of this Court are to form part will exist and labor for the benefit and to the pride of the people, mark the death of this old, time-honored tribunal, and in the spirit of justice and kindness note its work and merits.

It is told that in some of the rural districts of Ireland a beautiful custom prevails which influences a traveler meeting a funeral procession, standing by the roadside, with head reverently uncovered, to lay upon the bier a wildflower or a few blades of grass, and so I, as this old Court is passing away, although regretting that I have no flowers of rhetoric with which to brighten and perfume, yet reverently pay my humble tribute of respect.

187

Our people are too much disposed in these days, to slight the work and sacrifices of holders of judicial and other offices, and too slow to accredit to those who serve the public in official stations, dispositions unselfish and for the public good.

Our Judges cannot be held in too high respect, our Courts in too high reverence, and we lawyers should be prompt in fostering such respect and reverence as well by our united expressions as by our individual professional action.

This occasion is full of interest to all of the citizens of this great metropolis, for in the march of progress which it has grandly made, the Court of Common Pleas has held an honorable place. You cannot take from the Court its past as a part of our municipal life and history. That "at least, is secure." Surviving until now, the changes of government, the vicissitudes of politics, and the dangers of constitutional conventions and judicial commissions, it has come down to us in this day with a record of usefulness and dignity which compels our admiration. There must have been in it much of merit to endear to the people this Court of Pleas, as it was designated in one of the old charters of the city, and of Common Pleas, as it afterwards became, calculated by its title alone to keep it in touch with the people, to warrant its long life. Its age and place alone entitle it to our respect.

But to us as lawyers there is additional and higher reason why we should be impressed with the importance and solemnity of this occasion. This is not only an *old* Court, but it is a Court of superior jurisdiction, upon the bench of which have sat distinguished Judges who have labored in the public interest, and made records spotless as to integrity and bright as to genius and industry. I may be pardoned reference to one who to our delight still passes among us, not at all as lingering on the stage of life, but with full strength, keen intellect and wit, full of charming reminiscence, entitled because of age, character, intellectuality and duty well performed, to the title of New York's first citizen, whose incumbency began before many of us were born. It were reason enough for these exercises that ex-Chief Justice Charles P. Daly, whose name and that of the Court will always be inseparably connected, is able to make us happy, as he has done by his presence among us.

And then, how the walls of these rooms and of the older Court rooms in the City Hall, have rung with the eloquent tones of the lawyers who in their day were the giants of the bar. Occasions like this are stopping places on the highway of professional life, and here pausing we look back over the road we have traveled. During more than a quarter of a century of active work in the Courts I have seen in those old rooms great lawyers who have passed away, whose learning and eloquence charmed both bench and bar.

Fame is at the best, transient and fleeting, human endeavor is often unappreciated, the good that men do often dies with them. Our words of to-day will soon be forgotten, and yet as in this ceremony we shall have performed in part our duty to this ancient and honorable Court, all who have taken part will feel that the day has been well spent.

The committee charged at the preliminary meeting

of members of the bar with the management of the exercises for this day, was directed to prepare a resolution appropriate to the occasion, to be, if adopted, here with your permission, placed upon the record of this Court. I am favored in being selected to present for your consideration this resolution:

As under the amended Constitution the Superior Courts of cities are to be consolidated with the Supreme Court of the State, the Court of Common Pleas for the City and County of New York will soon cease to exist as a separate branch of our judicial system,

Therefore we, members of the bar of the City of New York, place upon record this public expression of our respect for the Court, of our regard for its Judges, and for the value of their labors; of our good wishes for them in the new field of duty to which the Constitution calls them; and of our gratification that in the entire history of the Court, which began with the dawn of this city's existence, there is no page that would be bettered by excision and erasure. The names of the Judges who have in the past sat upon its bench are inseparably connected with the development of the system of jurisprudence of this State which has been a guide to the Courts of the other States of the Union; and the steady increase of its business in the last few years is a convincing witness that to the very end the Court has grown in the confidence of the bar and the people of New York. The Court of Common Pleas for the City and County of New York will live in the good work that it has finished, and in pleasant recollections of its courtesy, its dignity, its usefulness and its uprightness.

ADDRESS OF EX-CHIEF JUSTICE CHARLES P. DALY.

MR. CHAIRMAN: As this Court will go out of existence to-morrow, I have been asked by the chairman of the committee who has had the arrangements for this meeting in charge to give an account of how it came into existence, with such other historical matter respecting it as might be interesting and appropriate. I have agreed to do it, but shall do so very briefly, as there are several other gentlemen present who are to address the meeting.

Lawyers who have given any attention to the system of jurisprudence we inherited from England know that after the Norman conquest there was in England a great Court called the Aula Regis. It was a Court held by the king, or, in his absence, by an officer called the Chief Justiciary, assisted by the principal officers of State and such barons as were summoned to attend it, in the hall of the king's palace, for a certain number of days called a term, in the periods of Christmas, Easter and Whitsuntide in whatever part of England the king at that time might be; in other words, it was a part of the king's household. It was held with great pomp and ceremony, especially when the king presided in person, which William the Conqueror frequently did, sitting with his crown upon his head and upon a high bench, more elevated than the seats around him, from which we get the term in use to the present day of the "bench."

The chief business of this great Court, the highest in the realm, was of two kinds that were distinguished from each other by the terms "Pleas of the Crown" and "Common Pleas:" the Pleas of the Crown embracing crimes and misdemeanors, all matters relating to the revenue, and all other matters in which the government was interested, while Common Pleas were disputes or complaints between individuals in which was included all questions relating to land or what was called real actions, which was at that time the chief subject of litigation. Now the largest part of the business that came before the Aula Regis was that coming under the head of common pleas, or what we now call "civil actions," and it was felt to be a great hardship that the suitors in such actions had, for the determination of them, to go before the King's Court, in whatever part of England that Court might be. It was one of the grievances presented on behalf of the people when Magna Charta was wrung by the barons from King John and which was removed by a clause in that great charter declaring "that Common Pleas are not to follow the king, but are to be heard in some certain place." This provision led in the reign of Henry III., about or very near the year 1234, to the breaking up of the Aula Regis into two Courts, creating a separate Court which was permanently fixed in London for the trial of common pleas, and to which the name was given of the "Court of Common Pleas."

In the reign of Henry's successor, Edward I., justly called by Coke, the English Justinian, the Aula Regis, as such, was abolished and a new Court formed in its place with nearly the same jurisdiction as a legal tribunal, to which the name was given of the King's Bench; and, to distinguish the King's Bench from the Court of Common Pleas, the latter for some time, or occasionally, thereafter was called the Common Bench, but its original name remained of the Court of Common Pleas, and it continued to be called by that name until it ceased to be a separate tribunal.

The establishment of this tribunal which was fixed permanently in London led to very important results. It has been said that we owe to it the preservation of the common law. The administration of the law before that time was chiefly in the hands of the ecclesiastics, who were trained in the civil and canon law, and they were gradually substituting that foreign system for the common law to which the people were deeply attached. The establishment, therefore, in the language of Stephens the commentator, "of this principal Court of Common Law at that particular period and at that particular place, gave rise to the Inns of Court which collected together in London all the common law lawyers of England, and by which the common law was enabled through their influence and firmness to stand all the attacks made by the canonists and civilians who sought to destroy it;" and all those who value the liberty enjoyed in this country and in England and which has been secured by the common law, will feel how great that service at that particular period was. Of all the higher Courts, the Court of Common Pleas was for centuries the popular Court and had among its Judges some of the most distinguished names in the history of English jurisprudence. I will not now stop to repeat those names. It is sufficient to mention two of them, Coke and Eldon.

The Court existed for 641 years when it was amalgamated with the other higher Courts in 1875, retaining however its historical name as the Common Pleas Division.

When this city, in 1664, was taken from the Dutch by the English, the commander of the English expedition and the first governor of the province thereafter known as New York, found a court established here called the "Worshipfull Court of the Schout, Burgomaster and Schepens" which had been in existence from 1653—242 years ago: the Schout being equivalent to our Sheriff, Burgomaster to our Mayor, and Schepen to that of Aldermen, which Court combined the twofold qualities of a municipal body for the local government of the city and of a Court of Justice having both civil and criminal jurisdiction. Governor Nicolls altered the name of the city from New Amsterdam to New York, and gave the same name to the province, which, before that, had been known as New Netherlands. He desired also to convert this important Dutch Court as far as he could into an English tribunal. The task was not an easy one. All the proceedings were conducted in the Dutch language. The Court, therefore, had to be conducted as before under the Dutch law and in the Dutch language which it was for many years thereafter under the governorship of Colonel Nicolls and of his successor Lord Lovelace. But Nicolls determined to do something, at least, to give it as far as possible an English character, and as he was a soldier, and not a lawyer, he no doubt availed himself of the assistance of Matthias Nicolls an English lawyer, who had settled in New Amsterdam before it was captured by the English. One might naturally ask what an English lawyer could find to do professionally in this little Dutch town, as New Amsterdam then was; but he had been employed by the Dutch governor, Stuyvesant, in his controversies with the New England colonies, and as there was considerable trading between the inhabitants of these eastern colonies and the Dutch capital, there may have been professional business for an English lawyer. He was in fact such a useful and capable man that Governor Nicolls shortly after he took possession of the city, made him Secretary of the Provinces, which he continued to be until the city was retaken by the Dutch in 1673. He was a well informed lawyer, and he no doubt suggested to the Governor that all he could do was to give English names alike to the Court and its officers, and also what those names should be. As the Court was permanently fixed in the City of New York it would naturally occur that, as in this respect it was more like the Court of Common Pleas, which was permanently fixed in London, than any other English Court, and as a large part of the business it transacted was of the same kind, questions or controversies between individuals, an appropriate name for it would be the Court of Common Pleas. But it had also what the English Court of Common Pleas had not, a criminal jurisdiction in respect to offences occurring in the city; and as in this respect it was like the Mayor's Court of London, a proper English name for it also would be the Mayor's Court, and that this could be further carried out by changing the name of Burgomaster to that of Mayor, Schepen to that of Alderman, and of Schout to Sheriff, making the Mayor, and not the Sheriff, as the Schout had been in the Dutch Court, the chief presiding officer, all of which was done; and for many years thereafter it was known by either name as combining the function of both of the two London Courts, the Mayor's Court and the Court of Common Pleas.

After this change was made, Gov. Nicolls appointed as the first Mayor of New York, Thomas Willet, an Englishman, who was thoroughly acquainted with the Dutch language, having been employed previously by Stuyvesant in important negotiations. He was a man of ability, firmness and integrity, whose direct descendant, as I saw by the newspapers a month or two ago, died in Jersey City at the advanced age of 90; and, Willet with the exception of introducing the trial by the jury, carried on the Court as it had been before, under the Dutch law and in the Dutch language.

Another feature was afterwards added to the Court. In the Mayor's Court in London it was found as the Mayors were generally laymen and frequently changed, they were not well informed in respect of the law, and that it was necessary to have a permanent officer who was well acquainted with it attached to the Court, who could assist the Mayor, and who would see that the records of the Court were properly kept; and, for that purpose, the office of Recorder was created, and that officer thereafter sat with the Mayor as a permanent member of the tribunal to whom the Mayor could refer when any question or doubt arose respecting the law. This was thought to be also desirable in New York; and in 1683 the corporation of the city sent a petition to Gov. Dongan for certain municipal changes, among the rest that a Recorder might be appointed to assist the Mayor in the Mayor's Court, which the Governor granted, and appointed James Graham, who was one of the petitioners, Recorder. He was a Scotchman who came to the Colony in 1678, and Mrs. Lamb in her "History of the City of New York," says of him that "he

RUFUS B. COWING.

ROBERT A. VAN WYCK.

JAMES G. O'GORMAN.

GEORGE F. ROESCH.

was the second son of the Marquis of Montrose;" that "he was endowed with brilliant intellectual qualities, was witty, chivalrous, communicative; overflowed with anecdote; that he was a lawyer who had already attained distinction at the bar, and a man of great dignity; of fine presence and a master of rhetoric, who in his tastes, habits and methods of thought, was a fair type of the ancient nobility of Great Britain."

This is a fine picture of an attractive and very accomplished man; but not one word of it is true. The Marquis of Montrose had no second son, and Lord Bellamont, who was then the Governor of the Province, in one of his letters to the Board in London that had the affairs of the Colony in charge, says that Graham was bred to a trade and neither to learning nor to the law, which he gives as the reason of his incompetency in the two offices which he held, of Attorney-General and Recorder. He never attained any distinction whatever at the bar, and procured those offices entirely through personal and political influence. On the contrary, Lord Bellamont says that the government lost many cases through Graham's inability as Attorney-General to draw up the papers properly; and Parmentier, who was an educated and well-read lawyer, ridiculed Graham for his ignorance of the law. As to his brilliant intellectual qualities, a master of rhetoric, witty, chivalrous, a man of fine presence and of great dignity, I have in my researches found no allusion to any of these characteristics. Mrs. Lamb refers to none; and finally, in respect to this first Recorder of the city of New York, Lord Bellamont removed him from the office of Attorney-General and Recorder because he was incompetent and corrupt.

To follow the history of the Court from this period to the year 1823 would be to go over all the Mayors and Recorders who sat in it as Judges. It will suffice to say that many of them were distinguished men, such as Edward Livingston, the author of the penal code of Louisiana, Chancellor Kent, Chief Justice Jones, Jacob Radcliffe, Judge Josiah Ogden Hoffman, De Witt Clinton, Cadwalader D. Colden. and Peter A. Jay. In the year 1823 it was felt that the presiding or Chief Judge who had theretofore been the Mayor on the civil side of the Court, ought to be a lawyer, for out of the thirty-five Mayors who up to that time had presided in it as Judges, only three of them had been lawyers. Accordingly in that year, an act was passed creating what was called the First Judge of the Court of Common Pleas, who was required to be of the degree of counsellor-of-law, and John T. Irving, a brother of Washington Irving, was appointed, who was still on the bench when I came to the bar fifty-eight years ago. The effect of this was that thereafter the Recorder presided in the criminal part of the Court, or, as this was afterwards called, the Court of Sessions, and Judge Irving sat in the civil part thereafter known only as the Court of Common Pleas. The Recorder and the First Judge could lawfully sit in either Court, but neither did, and practically, they became separate tribunals. Judge Irving was so highly esteemed by the bar as a Judge that the business in his branch of the Court increased so largely, that in 1834, an Associate Judge was created, to which position Michael Ulshoeffer was appointed, and when Judge Irving died in 1838, after being upon the bench for seventeen years, an act was passed by which another associate Judge was created, and Judge Ulshoeffer became First Judge, and Daniel P. Ingraham was appointed Associate Judge. The business grew still greater, and in 1839, another Associate Judge was created, Wm. Inglis was appointed, who was my immediate predecessor. The Court then consisted of three Judges which by the Constitutional Amendment of 1867 was increased thereafter to six Judges.

I have now, sir, done what I agreed to do, brought the history of the Court down to the time that I became a member of it, which I was for forty-two years. Of that period in its history, it is more befitting that another than myself should speak. I might with propriety refer to the many distinguished lawyers now passed away, who came before me during that long period, and as a survivor, pay my tribute to their memory by pointing out their distinguishing characteristics, either as lawyers, or as advocates. It would be a pleasant exercise of memory to recall the displays I have witnessed of forensic eloquence, of intellectual power, of legal acuteness and legal learning, of the adroitness, skill and ability with which cases were managed, and the tedium of trial relieved by flashes of wit or an advantage gained by a telling sarcasm; but to do so would exceed the time I have prescribed to myself.

Of course, sir, I cannot realize without some feeling, that a Court will cease to exist to-morrow, in which so many years of my life were passed, in which I have seen such displays of legal ability, and I might say genius, of which I have so many memories both of lawyers and of Judges. Of the eighteen Judges who were associated with me in the Court, seven only now survive, and of the lawyers who came before it and have now passed away, I recall many, who in natural endowment, legal knowledge and legal training, would in any country where the law is cultivated and respected, be regarded as distinguished ornaments of their profession. All of them I knew personally; some of them most intimately; and when at my advanced age I recall what they were in the forensic arena, the charm of their society in private life, with all the associations and memories of my past professional career which an occasion like this awakens, I may in closing my remarks give adequate expression to it by quoting a verse of a well-known song of the poet Moore:

> " I feel like one who treads alone
> A banquet hall deserted;
> Whose lights are fled, whose garlands dead
> And all but he departed."

ADDRESS OF MR. WILLIAM ALLEN BUTLER.

I beg leave to second the resolutions which have been offered by my brother, McClure. The intervening history of the Court, to which we have just listened, adds additional interest to the dignity of this occasion. Ten years ago this very day, December 30th, 1885, at this very hour, and in this very place, the members of the bench and bar assembled to give expression to their respect for Chief Justice Charles P. Daly on his retirement from the bench of this Court (with which he had been connected for a period of nearly fifty-two years) under a mandate of the Constitution which limited his term of service. After a decade he is, happily, here with us, a witness to the retiring of the Court itself under the mandate of the present Constitution which has decreed its extinction as a separate branch of the judiciary of this State and city, and summoned its Judges to another sphere of judicial labor. In the expiring hours of this year, we are closing a most important and interesting chapter in the annals of our jurisprudence, and we are here with one accord, so far as it is in our power, to set the stamp of approbation upon the completed record of this Court.

It is altogether fitting that the event be thus solemnized. What the ex-Chief Justice has read as the result of his researches and the fruits of his memory, while it may not have been beyond the knowledge of some of us as to the origin and course of development of this Honorable Court, was none the less instructive and interesting.

The familiar designation of the "Common Pleas" had its origin in an early period of the jurisprudence of England. Sir Edward Coke claimed for the Court of Common Pleas an existence ante-dating Magna Charta. Lord Campbell assigns its origin to the reign of Edward I., "the English Justinian," in the latter part of the thirteenth century. From that time it has held its place as the title of one of the great judicial departments of Great Britain and in the recent reorganization of the English Courts the time-honored appellation is perpetuated in the "Common Pleas Division." With us, the name of "Common Pleas," long ago adopted and naturalized as designating a part of our judicial system, is a familiar sound, interwoven with all our studies of the law as a science and with all our practice at the bar. Courts of Common Pleas in the different counties of the State as they existed in the Colonial days, were continued by the Revised Statutes for many years. But especially was the "Common Pleas" a household word in our municipality, with a touch of homlier significance than ever belonged to the terms "Superior" or "Supreme" because more nearly kindred to the common interests and rights over which it threw the imperial ægis of the law.

Speaking for the older members of the bar, I may be permitted to recall the associations of this Court with the City Hall, which has been more fortunate in escaping a projected transplantation. An outgrowth of the Mayor's Court, and including that official, the Recorder and the Aldermen among its nominal members, the proper place for the sitting of the Court of Common Pleas was the chief municipal building and it was in the City Hall that its terms were held. During its residence there and after it had outgrown connection with the city officers and was composed of its own Judges, it attracted to itself that large share of important litigations which it has always retained. My earliest professional recollections of the Court are associated with Judge Ulshoeffer and Judge Ingraham as its presiding Judges, and with such leaders of the bar as James T. Brady, James W. Gerard, Francis B. Cutting, Charles O'Conor, and that admirable lawyer whose peculiar field of practice was the Common Pleas, Augustus F. Smith. I well remember one of my own first cases, a very notable one, before Judge Woodruff and a jury in which, during a protracted trial, the legal acumen of Marshall S. Bidwell, Daniel Lord and Benjamin F. Butler were supplemented by the matchless forensic eloquence of Ogden Hoffman. True, he strayed off, to my dismay, on the eve of his summing up, to a Saint Nicholas dinner, leaving me to spend the midnight hours on a brief whose dry details he transmuted into a golden current of speech by the magic of that native gift of persuasion in which he " snatched a grace beyond the reach of Art." If I had taken any exception to his treatment of myself it was cured by the verdict. I might name others who are familiar to my recollection. But they have passed away. When the Court was removed to this Court House, many whom I see here to-day will, with me, bear witness to the unvarying courtesy, the strict integrity and the conspicuous ability with which Chief Justice Charles P. Daly administered the law, and to the exhibition of the same qualities by those who have occupied the bench of this tribunal.

Perhaps we ought not to be unmindful that such incidents as the passing away of Courts are no novelties in our juridicial history. Since my own admission to the bar, in 1846, I have witnessed the extinction of the Court of Errors, a tribunal modeled after the highest Appellate Court of England and coeval with the beginning of our constitutional government. The Court of Chancery with all its immemorial associations and vast powers, went out of existence at the same time; both of these time-honored tribunals were swept away by the tide of legal reform but not oblivion. The authority of their decisions was never more controlling than to-day; and they enshrine the names and memories of such jurists as Spencer and Bronson, Verplanck, Kent and Walworth. So it will be with this Court. It will hold its place in history; its Judges will hold their place in the long line of judicial succession. With our natural regrets at the termination of its existence we can only hope that the new departure to follow in our judiciary system may be a step forward in the onward march of American civilization. In any event, we are sure that you, Mr. Chief Justice and your associates on the bench, will carry with you the respect and esteem of the bar of this city and that in your new sphere of service there will be no lowering of the high standard of judicial integrity and ability which will always be imperishably linked with the now historic Court of Common Pleas.

ADDRESS OF MR. WM. B HORNBLOWER.

MR. CHAIRMAN AND BRETHREN OF THE BAR:—After what has been said so well and so eloquently by my brother, Butler, and after the remarks that have been made by the late Chief Justice of this Court, and after the resolutions that have been so forcibly and eloquently presented by my brother McClure, my task is indeed a simple one; I can but echo what has already been said. My recollection of this Court does not extend back further than the judicial life of the present Chief Justice of the Court. I tried my first case in this Court before one who is still a member of the bench of this tribunal, and I can therefore speak of the history of the Court only from what I have heard and learned from the reports and from the traditions of the bar. The traditional, conservative spirit of our profession has hitherto spared this Court from demolition. We cling tenaciously to old forms and old names; and we do so because we believe—and experience has shown—that old forms and old names have their value. But we get tired of being asked the continual question from our clients, and the world at large: Why do you do this? Why do you retain these Courts? Why do you have a Court of Common Pleas and a Superior Court and a Supreme Court? All with the same jurisdiction, except for certain technicalities which it defies the most astute lawyer sometimes to find out; and so when the profession is finally wearied of answering the question, why, they yield to the popular sentiment and allow the old landmarks to be swept away. But, sir, it is eminently appropriate that, when such a constitutional change in the judiciary system of the State is about to take place, some public notice of the change should be taken by the members of the bar. It is especially fitting that when this change involves the passing out of existence of two of the principal Courts of this city and county—the Court of Common Pleas for the City and County of New York and the Superior Court of the City of New York—that a tribute should be paid by the younger as well as the older members of the bar to the past records of those Courts on behalf of the bar and the community.

These two courts, sir, have become part of the history of this city and county and they will remain part of that history, and their decisions will remain part of the jurisprudence of this State for all time to come.

205

This Court of Common Pleas traces its record back, as we are told by the venerable ex-Chief Justice of the Court who still lives and moves among us, far beyond the foundations of the republic. My function to-day is not to relate the history of this Court. I shall refer—and I trust I may do so without invidious comparison—to one period in the history of this Court which has always made a great impression on my mind; I refer to that period covered by the Reports of E. D. Smith, containing the opinions of that strong triumvirate then in the prime of early manhood—Judges Ingraham, Daly and Woodruff. The four volumes of E. D. Smith's Reports, I do not think can be matched anywhere for terse, vigorous, lucid and accurate statements of the principles of law. They will be found cited in the Court of Appeals Reports, I believe, more frequently than any other reports of the purely local Courts. Of that triumvirate, one—Judge Ingraham—became afterwards the Presiding Justice of the General Term of the Supreme Court for this department during the very stormy period of the history of the bench and bar; another—Judge Woodruff—subsequently served a term as a Judge of the Superior Court of the City of New York, and then, after a brief period of active practice at the bar, became a member of the Court of Appeals of this State and ended his career as Circuit Judge of the United States for the Second Judicial District, dying at the comparatively early age of sixty-three years, after a life of almost uninterrupted judicial labor; the third of the triumvirate, afterwards Chief Justice of this Court, is still with us, as has already been said, full of years and honors: no one can think and speak of the Court of Common Pleas without thinking of Charles P. Daly. Probably there are not a dozen men in this room who can remember the time when Charles P. Daly was not a Judge of the Court of Common Pleas. To this Court he gave, practically, the whole of his active life, retiring only when he had reached the constitutional limit of age, and then retiring with the respect and esteem of the entire profession. I shall not stop to enumerate the other distinguished Judges who have sat upon this bench, many of whom have subsequently adorned the benches of other Courts, some of whom are still living and two of whom are now able and useful members of the Supreme Court bench in this district. Nor would it be fitting that I should speak of those who now compose the membership of this Court, except to assure them, as has already been done, that they end their judicial careers in this tribunal with the thorough regard and respect of those who have had the pleasure of appearing before them, and that it is a source of satisfaction to us all to know that their services are not lost to the community and that they, as Justices of the Supreme Court will still continue to be useful and honored public officials. There are many things in the new judicial machinery of the Constitution of 1894, which I, for one, would have had otherwise. I regret, for instance, that the Constitution has, by a hard-and-fast rule prevented us from availing ourselves of the judicial ability found among the Judges of these two Courts for use in the Appellate tribunal. But constitutional changes always work some injustice and hardship and some temporary evils. It has been pointed out by the ex-Chief Justice, and Mr. Butler, that the prototype of this Court—the Court of Common Pleas of Great Britain—traced its warrant from the Magna Charta, and so as this Court goes out of existence we desire to put upon record our tribute of respect and to assure them that they have followed in the footsteps set them by the eminent Judges of that tribunal whose name they bore and we desire to express our hearty good wishes to the members of the Court who pass to the Supreme Court and before whom we hope we shall be privileged for many years to come to practice in behalf of our clients and from whom we know that we shall always receive patient, careful and conscientious hearing.

ADDRESS OF MR. EDWARD LAUTERBACH.

MR. CHAIRMAN AND GENTLEMEN:—There is an air of solemnity in these proceedings which I think is by no means justified by the facts.

The nomenclature of the Court of Common Pleas is to be lost; its rules, which varied in some respects from the rules of other Courts, will no longer exist; the allotment of the Judges will be to special functions somewhat differing from those heretofore exercised; but the spirit that has animated the Court of Common Pleas and served to make it in public estimation what it is, its kindness and indulgence, its fairness and impartiality, its high tone and dignity will be carried with it and with its Judges into the new sphere of activity to which they have been transferred by recent constitutional provisions.

There is not to be an absorbtion or elimination of

t his Court's best attributes. An apotheosis is to take place—a translation from one realm to another, neither higher nor greater though somewhat different.

When the Court of Common Pleas, with its untarnished record, its ancient and interesting history, and all that has endered it to us above and beyond all others, becomes assimilated with another kindred tribunal, its individuality will tend to strengthen it, to fortify it, to add to its merit and happily without the extinction of any of those of its own distinguishing characteristics which have made the Court of Common Pleas for the City and County of New York the idol at least of the younger if not of all the members of the New York Bar.

No one more fitting to have delivered the principal address of the day than the nestor of our bar, Mr. William Allen Butler, could have been selected, for his career conjoined with that of his illustrious father, Mr. Benjamin Franklin Butler, the leader of the bar in his day, are coincident almost from the beginning to the very end with that of the Court in whose presence we now stand.

The addresses already made, the interesting history of the Court contained in the monograph which opens the first volume of E. D. Smith's Reports, and which is the result of the scholarly research of Mr. O'Callaghan and of the eminent former Chief Justice of the Court, supplemented as it is by the statement which the latter has just read to us, renders any further historical allusion or panegyric unnecessary.

It is, I assume, that as a representative of those members of the bar to whom this Court has been most helpful by encouragement and by precept, those to whom admission to its portals was not accorded by the law school diploma, those whose struggling steps were unaided by special tuition and whose path to the cherished goal was not rendered easy by well qualified pedagogues and professors, those whose earlier experience after admission was limited more particularly to that acquired in the District Courts and in the former Marine Court, now the City Court, that I am called upon to express on their behalf the sincere gratitude owing by them to this Court for its special and thoroughly appreciated interest in their behalf.

Possessed of sole and final appellate jurisdiction in this class of cases it was here that swift redress from injustice to the litigant in these lower Courts, not always presided over, as is now the case, by men of ability and fairness, could be and was readily obtained; but what was of more consequence than their affirmance or reversal, was the knowledge that every case, however lowly the parties in interest, however trifling the amount involved, would secure patient and attentive consideration, and the young advocates of these causes the same generous treatment as was afforded to their leaders in the more important branches of the law.

On behalf of these, hundreds of whom owe subsequent successful careers mainly to the encouragement so received, I bear a message of most sincere, earnest and heartfelt thanks and gratitude to, and of love and affection for the present members of this Court and their predecessors.

Nor do we fail to remember the contrast which was afforded by this Court during the period to which reference was made to-day when other tribunals were unduly affected by political influences.

Never shaken in its serenity, never unmindful of judicial propriety and judicial decorum, unswerved by political power or influence, the temptations to the youthful practitioner to yield to the methods then prevalent was the more readily shunned because of the rigid standard of professional and judicial honor here maintained.

When the Constitutional Convention of 1894, of which I had the honor to be a member, was convened, the spirit of reform so widely prevalent and which had for its cardinal principle the accomplishment of changes from existing conditions, whether for the better or for the worse, became rife at its sessions, and to such an extent that it was seriously mooted not only to abolish the Superior Court and the Court of Common Pleas, but to terminate the terms of office of their incumbent Judges.

Happily this spirit was of but short duration, and it was generally conceded that the *personnel* of all the Judges and the high repute of those Courts, justified a consolidation of the Courts without the curtailment of any term of office.

Consolidation was doubtless essential. From various causes differences of procedure prevailed, which might have been removed, but vital differences in jurisdiction and in power, some of which could only have been adjusted by constitutional amendment also prevailed, which subserved no useful purpose, and which tended greatly to vex, annoy and confuse the practitioner and the litigant, and so, for these and other reasons, the consolidation was effected, and wisely effected.

It may be doubted whether the limitations placed upon the transferred Judges in the exercise of judicial functions in the newly created Court were wise. Certainly nothing in the individuality of these Judges justified any discrimination, but this is after all only a minor matter, though regrettable, and arose not from a desire to make an invidious distinction among the Courts, but from the necessity of the creation of a larger Appellate tribunal, occasioned by the commendable abolition by the convention of the limitation of appeals to the Court of Appeals to judgments of more than five hundred dollars, which will increase the volume of business of the Court of Appeals and to the unwillingness of the convention to afford relief to that Court either by addition to its numbers or by providing for a Second Division of the Court in the event of any exigency. Membership in this Appellate Division, it was not unnaturally provided, should at the outset be confined to existing Judges of the Supreme Court.

You gentlemen who now constitute this Court wherever you may be, whatever tribunal you may grace, in whatever circumstances you may find yourselves, rest assured that our appreciation for you will never be less than it always has been; greater it cannot be.

ADDRESS OF SURROGATE JOHN H. V. ARNOLD.

MR. CHAIRMAN AND GENTLEMEN:—I do not rise here for the purpose of supplementing or endeavoring to supplement by any language of my own what has been so well said by the eloquent speakers to whom we have

listened, on the lines they have pursued. Every encomium which has passed from their lips must meet a
ready response in the breast of every citizen of New
York. The services of the long line of distinguished
jurists who have dignified and graced the bench of the
Court of Common Pleas through so many years must
be accorded that meed of praise which belongs to earnest and painstaking work, conspicuous ability, unim-
peachable integrity, devoted to public service. I rise
simply for the purpose of recalling on this interesting
occasion, to which it may be appropriate, the associations which have long existed between the Surrogate's
Court of the City and County of New York, of which I
have the honor to be a representative, and the Court of
Common Pleas. And I shall do so very briefly and I
know very imperfectly. We are told by the learned
Chief Justice to whom we have listened with so much
pleasure here to-day, that the Mayor's Court of New
York, which was in a sense a predecessor of this Court
for a considerable period exercised jurisdiction over
the probate of Wills and grants of letters of administration, and over the settlement of estates; and many
Wills involving titles to valuable real estate in this city
and county, were probated in that Court, and were to
be found among its records. It was then not at all
unnaturally, although perhaps not due at all to that circumstance, that, when provision was made in the
statutes of this State for the filling of a vacancy caused
by death of the Surrogate, the duty of filling that
vacancy, for the time being, was assigned to and
devolved upon the Court of Common Pleas. And it
was while serving as temporary Surrogate upon the

death of Surrogate West, that the learned Chief Justice of this Court in the matter of the Brick Estate, for the first time set forth clearly and succinctly the history of the Probate Courts of this State, of the powers and jurisdiction which they had exercised, and their sources, subjects which were involved at that time in very much of obscurity, in fact had been substantially pronounced both by bench and bar as untraceable. He pursued his labors on those subjects with assiduity and prodigious industry, reaching in every case plain and incontrovertible conclusions. His work was commended most gracefully by the Court of Appeals, as evincing a patience and accuracy of research which left nothing to be added; and without doubt his work in this respect gave a great impetus to that legislation which subsequently followed and by which was inaugurated the comprehensive system of procedure which now governs and directs the Surrogate's Courts of this State, where before all was crudity and imperfection. Provision has also been made in the statutes of this State for the transfer of certain issues of fact arising in the Surrogate's Court, for trial by jury in the Court of Common Pleas, also for the exercise by the Court of Common Pleas of the powers and jurisdiction of the Surrogate's Court in cases of absence, sickness, disability and disqualification on the part of the Surrogate, and, as occasion has arisen, that jurisdiction and power has been so exercised. But there has been a very important class of cases arising out of contests of Wills originating in the Surrogate's Court which under provisions of law have been transferred to this Court for jury trial. The despatch of those cases has involved a great deal of additional labor on the part of the Judges of this Court. That labor has been assumed by them cheerfully, and always performed most satisfactorily and to the great relief of the Surrogate, and those services were rendered at times when their own business pressed heavily upon them. The Justices of this Court are entitled to the gratitude of the Surrogates, and I know that in tendering my acknowledgment of the same to them now upon this occasion, I speak not only for my associates and myself, but for my learned predecessors in the office.

The Judges of this Court will take with them into their new sphere of action, our best wishes, and the trust that they will long continue to serve the public.

ADDRESS OF CHIEF JUSTICE RUFUS B. COWING, OF THE COURT OF GENERAL SESSIONS.

In order not to be prolix, but brief, and to keep my remarks within your indulgence and patience, I have jotted down a few sentences which I beg respectfully to read to you as remarks coming from the appropriate representative of a Court so recently in the past associated with this.

The committee appointed by the bar to arrange the programme for this meeting has invited me as the senior Judge of the Court of General Sessions to be present and participate in its proceedings.

The new Constitution of our State has expressly decreed that on and after next Wednesday, the Court of Common Pleas shall cease to exist, and that its jurisdiction and Judges shall be transferred to the Supreme Court. We are assembled here to-day to take recognition of this fact and to, in some appropriate and formal way, record for all future time our respect and admiration for a Court which has in the past for so many years performed so conspicuous a part in administering justice in the State. We cannot fully appreciate the important part which this ancient and honorable Court has taken in administering the laws of the State without taking into consideration the varied extent of jurisdiction which its Judges have from time to time exercised.

It is not only a Court of very large and extensive original jurisdiction, but it has appellate jurisdiction in all cases on appeal from the City Court and the several District Courts of the city; and its Judges by statute are empowered to perform the duties of the Surrogate and also to preside in and over criminal trials in the Court of General Sessions. In the performance of the very pleasing duty assigned to me in this afternoon's proceedings I shall confine my remarks to a very brief review of the relation which this Court bears to the Court over which I have the honor to preside.

Over two hundred years ago the Court of Common Pleas and the Court of General Sessions were created, and have formed a part of the judicial system of the State ever since. While both Courts had at one time both civil and criminal jurisdiction, eventually the two Courts were reorganized, with distinct jurisdiction which they have since exercised: the Common Pleas for the trial of civil actions, and the General Sessions for the trial of criminal cases, although both tribunals were composed of the same persons. Up to the time

Ed Lauterbach

William Hildreth Field

F. R. Coudert.

of the granting of the Dongan Charter in 1686 the Mayor's Court was the principal Court of the Province, and exercised all the jurisdiction afterwards conferred upon this Court, and the General Sessions. In fact, the Mayor's Court not only at that time performed judicial duties but also legislative and executive. Without entering more minutely into the rise and progress of these two ancient and important Courts, let me say a few words in reference to my own.

The Court of General Sessions is in point of fact the highest criminal Court in the county. It disposes of over nine-tenths of the felonies committed and triable in the county, as well as many of the misdemeanors; and its importance in maintaining the peace and good order of society cannot well be overestimated. The Court, while it has not always been presided over by gentlemen learned in the law, has always been held in great respect by the people. For many years the Recorder was the only lawyer who presided over its trials, assisted by the Mayor and Aldermen; and this continued down to 1853 when by express law the Recorder and the City Judge were each empowered to hold the Court without the aid and assistance of either the Mayor or Aldermen. The jurisdiction of the Court is purely criminal and in this respect outranks all others except the Supreme Court, which is of co-ordinate jurisdiction. It has had upon its bench many men of great legal ability and distinction, among whom may be mentioned Recorders Riker, Hoffman and Smythe; and it has through its trials done very much in settling the criminal law and practice not only in this State but in the United States.

Without in any way desiring to detract from the great importance to the people of the civil jurisdiction of the Court of Common Pleas, in my judgment not the least, but the most important jurisdiction is that conferred by statute upon the Judges of this Court to preside over criminal trials in the Court of General Sessions. It is a jurisdiction which for many years has rarely been exercised, but nevertheless has at times been exercised with great ability and benefit to the public. It is a matter of congratulation that while the grand old Court of Common Pleas will soon go out of existence its jurisdiction and Judges will be transferred to a higher Court so that the people will still continue to have the benefit and advantage of the large experience and great ability of its Judges. A Court which has filled so large a place in the judicial system of the State for so long a period, which has accomplished such a vast amount of important judicial work, as is evidenced by its records and reports, which has had upon its bench so many distinguished and illustrious Judges and jurists, which has done so much to organize and perfect one of the most perfect and complete judicial systems of the world, needs no tablet to perpetuate its memory and fame. But so long as the memory of the present generation shall last, and recorded history shall continue to chronicle the rise and progress of our Nation and State, will the memory, fame and distinguished service of the grand old Court be handed down into the future.

I had jotted down some historical matters. But it is not my purpose to allude to them in any way, shape or manner. The learned Chief Justice has given a resume of all that need be said at this time; and I feel that for me to further trespass on your indulgence and patience at this hour would not only be cruel to you, but would be unjust to speakers, several of whom are to follow me. But I want to say to the Judges of the Common Pleas that I know they will carry with them the respect and confidence of all the members of the bar into that higher sphere of action into which they are to go; and while the name of "Common Pleas" will no longer be heard or mentioned except in reports and decisions, I am sure that the Judges themselves will always be remembered with the highest respect and gratitude for the services which they have performed to the people of this city and State.

ADDRESS OF CHIEF JUSTICE ROBERT A. VAN WYCK, OF THE CITY COURT.

We are gathered here to indulge in emotions of a conflicting character.

We recite with a fully justified pride the history of a Court rich in learning, presided over by learned jurists, and pregnant with far-reaching influences in the economy of this great metropolis.

While demonstrating a reason for its perpetual existence, we hear the mandate of our new Constitution proclaiming that the hour is reached when we must bid farewell forever to the Court of Common Pleas, which, however, will live in memory and form one of the brightest pages in the history of American jurisprudence.

The good-night to the Judges of the Court of Common Pleas is but the good-morning to the Justices of the Supreme Court, and the disappearing of the distinguished Chief Justice of the Court of Common Pleas, is but his immediate reappearance as Presiding Justice of one of the appellate branches of the Supreme Court.

The sorrows of death and the joys of birth, the sweet and the bitter, are strangely commingled in the thoughts suggested by these ceremonies.

The majesty of the commonwealth has decreed this change, and this is no time to question the wisdom thereof, for there is a sound philosophy in the proverb, "The king is dead, long live the king," which has an application to the situation.

However much we may esteem the dead ruler, or however much we may admire the old methods of the administration of any department of government, we must lend our best efforts to make successful the new ruler and the new method of administration, and it is the bounden duty of every Judge and lawyer to sincerely labor for the success of this new system of a consolidated Court for the administration of justice.

We justly boast of the long line of distinguished jurists who have adorned the bench of the Court of Common Pleas and we point with pride to the fact that their reported decisions have so frequently been cited by the Courts of the civilized world as binding authority by virtue of the innate strength of their reasoning and sense of justice, as to mark these Judges as richly endowed with both mind and conscience.

They manifested a sympathy and familiarity with human nature and the necessities of life, which always opens wide the broad avenues of knowledge and wisdom.

They seem never to have forgotten that law, in its nature, is the noblest and most beneficial of the sciences, but in its abuse and debasement the most sordid and pernicious.

They were the expounders of the law according to its reason and spirit, seeking to climb up to the vantage ground of the science, never attaching undue advantage to the mere technicalities, never extending hospitality to experts in the art of perverting and defeating the ends of justice.

To them the law was what it was designed to be, the science of justice, which defines the rights of person and property, interposing its powerful arm between the strong and the weak, and settling rights according to one uniform standard of even-handed justice to all.

They were the proud possessors of the confidence of the lawyers who are always sensitively jealous as to the maintenance of the purity of the judicial ermine.

No Court was ever freer from scandal and suspicion than this one; and it would indeed be less than human if the realization that it is to be no more, did not prompt the heart to sincere expressions of sorrow and regret.

Judges of the Court of Common Pleas, we bid you good-night. Justices of the Supreme Court, we salute you good-morning.

ADDRESS OF JUSTICE JAMES A. O'GORMAN, OF THE ELEVENTH DISTRICT COURT.

MR. CHIEF JUSTICE AND GENTLEMEN OF THE BAR:— This ceremony is unique because it is without a parallel in the annals of American law. We have been reminded by Mr. Butler of the dissolution of other Courts in the past, and especially of the Court of Chancery, and of the Court of Errors. But I venture to say that never before in any city upon this continent has a meeting of the bar been convened to take note of the passing away of a Court of Justice that could boast of an existence of two centuries and a half. The event is one of great significance, and marks an epoch in the administration of law in this State.

We have gathered here to-day not only to manifest our appreciation of the great ability that has ever distinguished the bench of this Court, but to express our regret that a Court with such an historic past, and with such grand traditions, should be swept away by a radical, and as many believe, an ill-advised change in our organic law.

The Court of Common Pleas of the City and County of New York is perhaps the most ancient American tribunal. It is twice as old as the Nation itself; and, measured by its antiquity, by the high character and professional attainments of its Judges, by its varied and important contributions to the jurisprudence of the State and Nation, by its long life of public usefulness, I think no Court in this State has a higher claim upon the confidence and commendation of the bar, and the citizens generally of this city. A contemplation of the history of this Court as reviewed for us to-day by the venerable Chief Justice, is well calculated to incite in us emotions of great and deep respect, and of admiration for this venerable tribunal. Dedicated as a temple of justice at a time when the population of this island numbered but a few hundreds, it has survived the

222

vicissitudes of wars and conquests, and for upwards of two hundred and forty-two years its force and power have been directed to the great end of human society— the administration of justice. We should be proud of this Court. No stain mars the beauty of its magnificent career. I know the bar of this city is proud of it. We are proud of its Judges, past and present. They have been in truth ministers of justice, always animated by a high and an exalted conception of their duties and responsibilities. To-morrow will witness the dissolution of this Court. But its record will live after it, and I am sure will always be prized by the bar of the city and county of New York as one of its most valuable possessions.

I second the adoption of the resolution.

ADDRESS OF JUSTICE GEORGE F. ROESCH, OF THE FOURTH DISTRICT COURT.

MR. CHAIRMAN, MEMBERS OF THE JUDICIARY AND OF THE BAR:—Through the courtesy of the Committee of Arrangements the Justices of the District Courts in our city are enabled to participate in this commemorative gathering.

These Courts will soon be the sole survivors of the ancient judicial system of our municipality. They can trace their lineage as District Courts, Assistant Justice's Courts and Justice's Courts as far back as 1759. True they are Courts of limited and purely statutory jurisdiction, yet they are peculiarly Courts of the poor people. Day after day the petty disputes of civic life seek adjustment in them, and even in these smaller forums questions of surprising magnitude often arise.

223

In the lower portion of our city the commercial strife of our metropolis is heard in them though upon a lesser scale than that which engages the attention of the higher Courts. In the upper portion large property interests are frequently at stake in the summary proceedings which are brought in them. On the great East side a dense cosmopolitan population crowds them with litigation which in frequency and intensity is in inverse proportion to the pecuniary amounts involved. The legal questions arising in these Courts in every portion of our city are fairly representative of the varied interests of the masses of our people. They rival in the importance of the results of their determination in the circles whose activities they affect, the larger judicial problems solved in the Courts of Record.

I listened gratefully to the eloquent language of the leader of the junior bar (Mr. Lauterbach) when he alluded to the importance of these minor tribunals. He did not overestimate the position they occupy and the rank they hold in our judicial life. But these Courts have not alone aided the people in the disposition of a great amount of petty litigation. They have been of service as well to the bar and the bench of our city. It has frequently been remarked that the Courts of Justice's of the Peace in our State have been nurseries of great men of our profession.

It can be asserted with equal confidence that the District Courts of our city have been the theatres of the early struggles and triumphs of men who have become famous at our bar, and who found in them excellent schools of forensic discipline. Nor must we forget that the District Courts have also been the cradles of great Judges who were transplanted from the lesser functions of these Courts to the higher sphere and more weighty concerns of the bench of the Court of Common Pleas. I refer to Hon. Fred. W. Loew and Hon. George C. Barrett, who in early life were occupants of the District Court bench and thus acquired valuable familiarity with the practical affairs of the every-day life of the common people.

It was indeed appropriate to invite these Courts to take part in these exercises. Since 1857 the General Term of the Court of Common Pleas was their appellate tribunal. It may be interesting to call attention on this occasion to the fact that during an interregnum of twenty-four days in the month of April in 1857, the appeals from the Districts Courts were directly to the General Term of the Superior Court of this city. I refer in support of my statement to the note in Day *v.* Swachhammer (5 Abb. Pr. Rep., 345). Shortly thereafter the old system was restored and the General Term of this Court has ever since had jurisdiction of appeals from the District Courts. Statistics will bear out the assertion that surprisingly few appeals are taken in comparison with the volume of business disposed of in the lower Courts. Last year about 200 appeals were heard though upward of 50,000 actions and proceedings were tried in the District Courts in that period of time. The most pleasant and cordial relations have subsisted between the Judges of the General Term of this Court and the Justices of the District Courts. We have always looked to you as our mentors and trusted and kindly judicial guides in the labyrinth of precedents and mass of principles in the law.

It is true that we part with you as a General Term. Yet we lose you in name only and we will not be deprived of the benefit of your example and influence. You will continue to blaze out for us among conflicting views those principles of justice which should be applied by us to the concerns of the people of our own Courts. We glory in the fact and congratulate ourselves upon the circumstance that in the Appellate Term of the Supreme Court in which the appeals from our Courts will be heard in the future there will be a trio of Judges intimately acquainted with the judicial life of these lesser tribunals and who understand the wants and needs of the people for speedy, cheap and substantial justice in these Courts.

I allude to Justices Daly, McAdam and Bischoff. No doubt they will follow as their polar star the spirit of the decision in Meyers *v.* Rosenbach (9 Mis. Rep., 89), in which Justice Pryor declares that " It is the distribution of substantial justice irrespective of formal rules of procedure that is the function of the District Courts in disposing of the litigation before them. Were they to be fettered by all the technical and recondite rules of practice with which Judges and counselors in Courts of Record are presumed to be conversant, they would surely miscarry in the attainment of that cheap and speedy justice which is the end of their institution."

We part with you, then, in name only. Your influence, your teachings and the benefit of your example remain with us. We will continue to entertain that veneration and esteem for you which have been the delight not only of the older but the younger members of the bar as well.

I know I voice the unanimous and heartfelt sentiment of my colleagues on the District Court bench when I express in their behalf the sincere hope that the lustre of your careers in your new and wider sphere of judicial activity may exceed, if possible, the renown of your noble past.

The resolutions offered by Mr. McClure and seconded were then put to vote by the chairman and adopted unanimously. The chairman then addressed the meeting.

ADDRESS OF CHIEF JUDGE JOSEPH F. DALY.

The Court of Common Pleas closes to-day a history co-extensive with that of the City of New York with which it has been so long identified. Its annals down to the year 1855, as prepared by its former Chief Judge, to whom we have had the great pleasure of listening to-day, form one of the most interesting chapters in local history. From 1855 to 1870 there was nothing to be added but the succession of its Judges; in the latter year it received a grant of constitutional powers which placed it for a quarter of a century in the first rank of State Courts.

My acquaintance with the Court began in the sixties, when a member of the bar. Its high reputation for the careful consideration of its cases and the learning and character of its Judges attracted a good share of the equity business of the profession although it had but three Judges and its law calendar was full. I commenced in it an action for an injunction to protect rights in real property and in that litigation I met for the first time the present Presiding Justice of the Supreme Court of this district. Our case was heard and determined by the then First Judge of the Court, Charles P. Daly. In 1870 we joined him upon the bench. A special Spring election of Judges was held in that year under the amended Constitution of 1869 reorganizing the Court of Appeals, the Supreme Court and Court of Common Pleas. Of the Judges then elected but three now survive, the Chief Judge of the Court of Appeals, the Presiding Justice of the Supreme Court of this district and the Chief Judge of the Court of Common Pleas.

The reputation of the Court of Common Pleas at the time of the Constitutional Convention of 1869 was such that with but three Judges and a calendar to which only about 350 cases were annually added, the Convention determined to extend its usefulness by doubling the number of its Judges. The new Judges were elected in 1870 and the next year the new issues added to its calendar were 968. Last year the new issues were over 1,300—the highest number in its history.

The increase was the more significant because the Court has had only five Judges to perform its work. Under the Constitution of 1870 the Governor was authorized to assign one or more of its Judges to assist in the work of the Supreme Court; and one of them has been so assigned continuously for twenty-five years. So that while its force was not quite double what it was in 1869 its business has trebled. But the provision for detailing its Judges to the Supreme Court tended, as was lately remarked by Mr. Carter, to the ultimate consolidation of the Courts. No matter how great the influx of cases to the Common Pleas the natural growth of business in the Supreme Court would tend to further drafts upon the judicial force of the former. In fact, in 1869 the Governor of the State communicated to us the request of the Supreme Court for the services of an additional Judge, a request which it was impossible to grant without injustice to our own suitors.

The consolidation of the local Courts of superior jurisdiction with the Supreme Court, which had been long discussed and which is now effected by the Constitution of 1894, grew out of no dissatisfaction with the work of these Courts. Had there been merely question of one good Court, or two of superior jurisdiction in the great cities, the reasons against consolidation might have prevailed; for, tested by the result of the scrutiny which the decisions of the several Courts undergo in the Court of Appeals, no Court of original jurisdiction fell far behind another in the quality of its work.

An examination of the Court of Appeals Reports for five years, from March, 1889, to April, 1894, gives the percentage of affirmances of the Supreme Court at seventy-five and of the Common Pleas at seventy-six, while those of the City Court of Brooklyn were still greater. An examination of the appeals in the years 1891 and 1892, made in the latter year and published at the time, showed that the reversals of the decisions of the Supreme Court and Common Pleas was only 5 per cent. in the former and 6 per cent. in the latter of the whole number of decisions rendered by their general terms and appealable to the Court of Appeals. If the observation of Dean Austin Abbott be correct that "an Appellate Court exists solely for the purpose of reversing," then the local Courts have added little to the labor of the Court of last resort.

Consolidation came, not from the necessity of improving the Courts of original jurisdiction—for, as ex-Judge Noah Davis recently said " the work of the Courts is now performed with an industry unparalleled in the history of the judiciary," but from the necessity of relieving the burdens of the Court of Appeals and to preserve that tribunal from unwieldy enlargement, or divisions into parts. To this end the system of intermediate appellate tribunals with final powers in certain cases, was devised; and that system required that the jurisdiction of all the existing general terms should be vested in those tribunals. It was perceived at once that all the advantages of separate independent local Courts would disappear with the consolidation of their general terms and the loss of control of their own judgments. One general term meant one Court notwithstanding that the forms of different organizations might be preserved. As the establishment of intermediate appellate tribunals necessitated the consolidation of the Courts, the change of system therefore began from the top; and the form of the trial Courts was changed in order to preserve the form of the Court of last resort.

The change was made by the framers of the new Constitution in a way to testify their respect for the local Courts and to remove all distinction between their

Judges and those of the Supreme Court, who were all to be assigned to the work of that Court without discrimination. The reason was not, as far as this Court was concerned, difficult to find. It was conspicuous in the record of its business. Its five Judges have held general terms, equity terms, trial terms and special terms in the exercise of jurisdiction co-extensive with that of the Supreme Court within the limits of this county. The general terms reviewed the appellate decisions of six Justices of the City Court, the judgments of eleven District Court Judges, and the judgments and orders of its own five Judges. The number of cases actually decided in the general term in 1871, when the additional Judges took their places was 284; it had increased in 1895 to 503; 384 written opinions were filed by the general term this year. In addition, the Judges tried 632 cases on the law, equity and special term calendars, heard 3,536 motions and made 14,040 *ex parte* orders.

It is significant that although the Judges with all possible application were able to dispose of but 391 causes on the jury calendar in 1894, new issues to the number of 1,305 were added to the calendar in that year; the Court having attracted business three times as great as its capacity to dispose of. In that year the insolvent assignment business of the Court aggregated 177 assignments with schedules showing over $3,000,000 of actual assets; and required at special term 118 final accountings and decrees and the making of 937 orders. The aggregate amounts involved in the business of the Court for certain periods needs no comment. The judgments in the Court for twenty years, to 1894, numbered over 20,000. The amount of the money judgments was $28,406,688; the amounts involved in mortgage foreclosures, $30,209,498; the insolvent estates actually distributed, $49,499,334.

This is the briefest possible glance at the work of the Court, work which the bar has been pleased to commend in to-day's proceedings. In performing day by day, with simple devotion, the duty nearest to them, the Judges have expected no reward like this; and they could desire no greater, It leaves us embarrassed for fitting words to reply. But I should not do justice to what I know to be the feelings of the whole bench of the Common Pleas, if I permitted this memorable occasion to pass without acknowledging the uniform courtesy which the Judges have received from the bar; and something more; for the bar of this city—noted as it has always been for the respect it pays to its judiciary—has unmistakably evinced towards this Court a warmer feeling.

Judges who respect the bar cannot fail to win its respect. When the bench appreciates the labors, anxieties, difficulties and responsibilities of the practitioner; sees in him, his cause and his clients; apprehends the consequences of litigation to the litigant and approaches the consideration of a case with a sense of its immense importance to the parties, there is no fear that the bar will fail to appreciate such conscientious feeling in the discharge of official duty.

It has been said that the bench of the Common Pleas has always kept in touch with the profession; that we have in a special manner shown the utmost consideration for its younger members. We have found them

ANDREW WARNER.   BENJAMIN H. JARVIS.

SAMUEL JONES.   ALFRED WAGSTAFF.

THE CLERKS OF THE COURT OF COMMON PLEAS.

deserving of it. We regard the future as full of promise for the profession in the ability and earnestness of its rising members. I alluded to the warmer feeling which the bar has entertained for this Court. On many occasions and by the voice of many of its members the profession has testified not merely respect, but affection, for the Court of Common Pleas. This we take with us as a priceless remembrance upon bidding farewell to the venerable institution which is now passing away and entering upon a new field of duty. We hope to carry with us your unchanged regard. Nothing will be altered but a form. As the ancient Court in the two centuries and a half of its existence saw generations of men as well as successions of Judges pass away, saw even governments and dynasties change, and survived them all, it seemed to be the substance and men but shadows. It now passes away with the shadows, but the substance remains. It will be strange indeed if all that made it respected and loved cannot be perpetuated in another form and in another tribunal. You can make your Courts and your Judges what you please. A courageous bar makes an incorruptible judiciary.

It now remains only to thank you, gentlemen, on behalf of the Judges of the Court for the honor you have done them in this commemorative meeting and in selecting the Chief Judge of this Court to preside over it. On behalf of the Judges of this Court I wish to thank the clerk, the assistant clerks, the stenographers and the attendants, for their assistance so long and faithfully rendered. Our last collective function is now to be performed. The Court which has existed for 250

years is to hold its last session.   Under the name of the
Court of Common Pleas, it has existed seventy-four
years and in that time has had twenty-three Judges.
Its first Judge, John T. Irving, sat in it seventeen
years; its second, Michael Ulshoeffer, sixteen years; its
third, D. P. Ingraham, twenty years; its fourth, Wm.
Inglis, five years, and its fifth, Charles P. Daly, forty-
one years, and he is with us to-day hale and vigorous.
Seven other Judges have sat in it for terms of eleven
to twenty-five years.   It has given five Judges to the
Supreme Court besides those now transferred; two to
the Superior Court and one to the Circuit Court of the
United States.   It has been closely connected with all
the local Courts and Judges and in performance of the
multifarious duties imposed upon it has furnished in its
reports authorities in almost all known proceedings;
and it closes its labors surrounded with that which
the poet says should accompany old age—

" As honor, love, obedience, troops of friends."

The prolonged applause following these remarks
having subsided,

The Chief Judge directed that the Court be convened
for the last time.

The crier, Mr. Thomas Sweeny, then formally
opened the Court.

Ex-Judge George M. Van Hoesen moved that the
proceedings of this meeting be placed upon the records
of the Court, and it was so ordered.

The Chief Justice then inquired if there was any
further business before the Court.

Whereupon the Clerk of the Court, Mr. Alfred Wagstaff, arose and said:

All the business submitted to the Court has been disposed of. The actions and proceedings pending will be transferred to the Supreme Court of this department of which the Judges of this Court are to be members. The seals, records, papers and documents belonging to the Court are ready to be deposited in the office of the Clerk of the County pursuant to the Constitution.

PRESENTATION OF A GAVEL TO CHIEF JUDGE JOSEPH F. DALY.

Mr. William S. Keiley, the Assignment Clerk, rose and addressed the Chief Judge. Mr. Keiley said:

To me, sir, has been assigned the pleasant duty, tinged though it be with a keen sense of sorrow at the severing of ties of friendship that have existed for about a quarter of a century,—of presenting to your Honor this emblem of your judicial power, which you have wielded so long and so faithfully, and with so much of honor and credit to yourself and this Court, and while we must accept it as an accomplished fact that the law of *gavelkind* cannot obtain in your Honor's case by reason of the constitutional demise of this Court,—still let us hope that the existence of this gavel may incite those who come after you to a laudable spirit of emulation—for, sir, in those dismal days when the judicial ermine in this country was befouled and an indignant people in their righteous wrath demanded reform, no breath of suspicion pervaded the atmosphere of this Court and the humblest litigant

235

here found a haven where the waters were pure, and the scales of justice were held with an even hand.

Accept it then, sir, in the same spirit which prompts its gift, as a modest token of that esteem and affection in which you shall ever hold a place in our memories— and be assured that though some of us less fortunate perhaps, than others, must seek our livelihood in other fields, yet to one and all it shall be the sweetest heritage to ever keep in fond memory the Court of Common Pleas and its last Chief Judge.

The Chief Judge replied as follows:

I am deeply touched by this remembrance, which I understand to be the gift of the senior and the assistant clerks of this Court, some of whom were already old in the service of the Common Pleas when, at an age so early as now to cause me as much wonderment as pride, I ascended its bench. If after so many years the veterans entertain so cordial a feeling for the youngest Judge under whom they ever served it is because he has ever held them in the same respect as when, as a young practitioner, he first knew them and recognized their functions as an essential part of the tribunal of justice; and because he never lost and never had occasion to lose his respect for the scrupulous care with which they performed their responsible duties.

It occurs to me, as I touch this gavel, that the bar will, perhaps, bear me out in saying that I have handled it more on this occasion than in the whole twenty-five years of my service on the bench. It was intended, I believe, to help me to enforce order. I never needed it. The decorum observed by the bar of New York is their distinguishing characteristic. But I

shall prize it for what it suggests. For, if the white-
ness of the ivory is figurative of the ideal judicial
character, let me say that the sterling gold of its
adornment is no less expressive of the character of our
bar.

Under the directions of the Chief Judge, the crier
then adjourned the Court of Common Pleas without
day.

INSCRIPTIONS UPON THE GAVEL.

On the gold band around the barrel was inscribed:

1653——1895.
1821 JOHN T. IRVING 1838
1838 MICHAEL ULSHOEFFER 1850
1850 DANIEL P. INGRAHAM 1858
1858 CHARLES P. DALY 1886
1886 RICHARD L. LARREMORE 1890
1890 JOSEPH F. DALY 1895

On one end of the barrel:

1870 to 1890 J.
JOSEPH F. DALY
1890 to 1895 C. J.

On the other end of the barrel: An impression of the
Court seal.

On the gold band around the handle:

This gavel was used
by the last Chief Judge
of the Court of Common Pleas
for the City and County of
New York.

HÆC OLIM MEMINISSE JUVABIT.

237

APPENDIX.

Extract from the New York Evening Post, Dec. 29th, 1885.

" Judge Daly was appointed to fill a vacancy by Governor
Bouck, under the old system, in 1844, and has been regularly
reëlected to succeed himself by the popular vote ever since. The
only time when he ran any risk of being dropped was in 1871,
when his term expired, and the Tweed Ring was well known to
need his place for a more pliant man. But its power had been
broken before the election came off, and he then was treated to
the great honor of a unanimous vote from all parties and factions
for the term of fourteen years which is now expiring. * * * * *

" What the general public is now called upon gratefully to remember is that Judge Daly has in his time sat in many great causes,
and passed on many great questions, often in troublous times, and
in times, too, when judicial integrity was much and reasonably
doubted, without ever having the shadow of a suspicion cast on
him by either victor or vanquished. It is this, after all, rather
than his legal learning, great as that may have been, which the
mass of his fellow-citizens have most prominently in mind to-day
in wishing him many happy years of well-won repose.

" It must also be said of him that at a period when the New
York bar is singularly absorbed in professional pursuits, when the
cultivation of other than professional knowledge is singularly
neglected by it, he has always found time for a reasonable devotion to literature and science. His services in geography and in
the promotion and elucidation of geographical research are known
to scientific men all over the world. He has been an industrious
investigator in many out-of-the-way historical fields, and in fact
so much so as sometimes to convert his judicial decisions into

genuine treatises, when the subject was one which admitted or called for this sort of discussion. Few Judges have, indeed, ever more fully illustrated the saying that 'the sparks of all other sciences are found in the ashes of the law.'

"In truth, during the last forty years there have been few literary or scientific movements in this city in which he has not taken a more or less prominent part, and few social gatherings of the intellectual kind at which he has not been a welcome and valued guest. He has in this way, too, reflected a sort of credit on the judicial bench. 'New York society,' as it is called, has not of late been as much indebted to the learned professions as it used to be in the days when Judge Daly was in his prime for the things which give refinement to wealth and luxury. Take him for all in all, we shall not soon see any one on the bench with such varied claims on general esteem and respect. It will probably be a long time before another Judge will appear who for forty-two years will fill the position with as little reproach, and win for it as much honor, and carry with him into his retirement so many friendly reminders that he has played well a great part."

Extract from the Daily Register, Dec. 30th, 1885.

"The Court of Common Pleas, in which he has so long presided, has, in reality, during the last half century, given the law to a very large portion of the inhabitants of this city on the subjects most closely connected with domestic and business welfare. Inheriting in some sense the limited functions and modest position of the Mayor's Court—an humble position in jurisprudence, when considered in relation to the general jurisdictions of the country—the Court of Common Pleas, under the administration of Chief Justice Daly and his associates, has carried forward the advances it has already made, and has steadily risen, winning, by growing public confidence, constant accessions of jurisdiction, until it now stands in coördinate rank with the Supreme Court, from which it differs simply by a few small territorial restrictions of jurisdiction.

"Those lawyers who have had a varied experience here will probably consider it no exaggeration to say that the controverted questions of law affecting more than half the population of the

240

city in respect to their homes, their contracts, their vocations, their tenancies and their business and social duties, have been sifted and settled in the Court of Common Pleas; and if of late in its appellate jurisdiction over the City Court it has had far more aid than in years gone by, undoubtedly it has formerly had at times no easy task in administering its appellate jurisdiction over the District Courts and the late Marine Court. The success with which it has held within practicable limits the constructions of law which those somewhat wayward tribunals were occasionally inclined to lay down, is no small element in the obligation which the city owes to the Judges of the Court of Common Pleas and their experienced chief.

"If it has not fallen to the lot of the Judge whose services we recognize, and whose return to the ranks of the profession we greet, to deal frequently with broad and far-reaching questions of constitutional law, public polity and criminal jurisprudence, it is because the public needs required him in the constant administrations of questions which come home still more closely to men's business and bosoms, and which though affecting fewer people than some of the litigations of the day, affect the parties and the local cummunity far more closely and vitally.

"The good sense and thorough research, the practical adaptation of learning to present necessities, the firmness and humanity with which his administration has been characterized deserves the recognition which the bar intends to give, and these qualities will continue to receive a growing appreciation as his opinions continue to be quoted and followed.

"No other Judge will probably deem it derogatory or beyond the limits of just recognition to say that to strike Judge Daly's decisions out from the body of our present authorities on the law of real property, landlord and tenant, carriers, master and servant, and contracts of employment, bailment, and hotel keeper's law, sales and negligence—not to mention other topics of scarcely less importance—would create as large an hiatus in our jurisprudence as the loss of those of any other Judge living or dead."

"It is not only on the bench that Judge Daly has used his legal knowledge in the service of the public. When the War of the Rebellion broke out he was a Democrat, but a true Union Democrat, always speaking in defense of the integrity of the Union and insisting that the rebellion must be put down at all hazards. He was in frequent consultation with President Lincoln and members of the Cabinet, who often sought his legal advice and generally acted upon it. When the crew of the rebel privateer 'Jefferson Davis' were convicted and sentenced to be hanged as pirates in 1861, Judge Daly met the President and his Cabinet and urged that they be pardoned and exchanged as prisoners of war. He reasoned that as a question of law there was no difference between the Southern soldier fighting the Union soldiers on land and the Southern privateer capturing our ships afloat. His arguments were so impressive that the President asked him to put them in the form of a letter, which he did, publishing it in the *Times, Herald, Sun* and *Tribune*. Three days after the President adopted his views and the prisoners were exchanged.

"A few evenings after the seizure of Mason and Slidell Judge Daly was dining with Chief-Justice Chase, when the question of the right to take them from a British vessel was discussed. The Judge was the only Democrat present, except Montgomery Blair. The feeling was universal at that time that the two rebel ambassadors ought not to be given up. Judge Daly's opinion was asked by the Chief Justice, and he promptly answered: 'I think we shall have to surrender them. Their seizure would be perfectly justifiable by the English law, but not by our own; I think that our cases are against us.' The Judge promised to hunt up the authorities, and he did so the next morning, finding a decision of Chief Justice Marshall that was flatly against holding the prisoners. He referred Secretary Seward to this, and that evening he saw William M. Evarts and told him his views. Mr. Evarts did not agree with him, but Mr. Seward evidently did, for four days after he published a letter consenting to the return of Mason and Slidell to the protection of the British flag. What might have happened had this decision of Judge Daly's, made in the face of strong opposition, not been accepted it is not pleasant

242

to reflect, now that the passions engendered by the war have passed away. At that time Sidney Bartlett, the eminent Boston lawyer, was the only person in Washington who agreed with Judge Daly on this important question of international law.

"The decisions rendered by Judge Daly during his long service in the Court of Common Pleas have been of a nature to reflect credit upon the court and himself. They have not only been written in the purest of English, so that they stand as worthy examples of American legal literature, but they show a vast amount of study and research, and information on special subjects, which testify to the care and labor which has been bestowed upon them. The Judge has found time in the midst of his arduous duties on the Bench to attend to many other things. In 1860 Columbia College conferred upon him the degree of LL. D. In 1867 he was elected a member of the State Constitutional Convention, and did valuable work on the Judiciary Committee, and on the Committee on the Submission of the Constitution. He has been the President of the Geographical Society for *twenty-two years*, and is an honorary member of the Royal Geographical Society of London, the Berlin Geographical Society, and the Imperial Geographical Society of Russia. He is almost as well known and as highly esteemed in Europe as in his native land. Alexander von Humboldt, to whom in 1851 he brought a letter of introduction from Chevalier Bunsen, then and for many years the Prussian Minister to England, said of him: 'Few men have left upon me such an impression.'"

The letters of Humboldt, to which reference is made both in the address of Mr. William Allen Butler and in the article from the New York *Times*, from which an extract has just been given, are from "Briefe Von Alexander von Humboldt and Christian Carl Josias. Freiherr Von Bunsen, Leipzig (F. A. Brockhaus), 1869."

Extract from Letter of July 18th, 1851.

" I cannot close these hurried lines without thanking you, from the bottom of my heart, for the acquaintance I made with Judge Charles Daly, from New York, who, upon his return from Italy, about a week ago, passed through here (Potsdam) and gave me almost a whole day of his time. All that you communicated to me about him, I have found confirmed in a much higher degree. Few men leave behind them such an impression of high intellect upon the great subjects that influence the march of civilization; in estimating the apparently opposite direction of character of those nations which surround the ever-narrowing basin of the Atlantic. Moreover, what is uncommon in a North American, and still more uncommon in the practical life of a greatly occupied magistrate, is that this highly intelligent and upright man has a deep and lively interest in the fine arts, and even in poetry. In my conversation with him about slavery, Mormonism and Canadian feudalism, I have directed his attention upon those questions which are especially interesting to me, particularly whether there is anything to be looked for with respect to the literature of a people, the noblest productions of whose literature have had their roots in another country."

Extract from Letter dated Potsdam, September 28th, 1851.

"Among the best men whose acquaintance I owe to you, I esteem Judge Daly, of the great State of New York, with whom I have had the opportunity of enjoying such important conversations."

THE HONORABLE WILLIAM INGLIS.

Since the writing and publication of the sketch of Judge Inglis, the following facts concerning his life have been definitely ascertained:

He was born December 27, 1804, and died May 29, 1863, in the 59th year of his age, and was buried in Trinity Cemetery, at 155th Street, in the City of New York.

He was the son of John Inglis, who was born in Scotland, March 26, 1763, and died December 6, 1848, aged 85 years. The family resided many years at Hoboken or Jersey City.

Judge Inglis was never married. His only surviving relative was a sister, Miss Margaret Inglis, who is still (1896) living in the City of New York.

FINAL PROCEEDINGS OF THE COURT OF
COMMON PLEAS.

A TRIBUTE TO THE COMMON PLEAS.

Extract from the New York Tribune (editorial), Dec. 27, 1895.

"The ancient Court of Common Pleas will not pass out of existence without a suitable commemoration of its past. With the
close of the year the Common Pleas and the Superior Courts will
be merged in the Supreme Court. It is fitting that suitable recognition of the honorable and distinguished part that the older of
these Courts has played in the jurisprudence of this city and this
community should be given. Arrangements have been made
with this object in view for a meeting in the General Term room
of the Common Pleas Court on next Monday afternoon. The
idea of holding such a meeting originated among members of the
bar, and, of course, lawyers will be the chief participants in the
celebration. But the event itself and the judicial history, the
memory of which it is intended to revive and perpetuate, are of
great interest to all the people of the city.

"It is natural that Chief Judge Daly* should be the central figure
of the occasion. For twenty-five years successively he has sat
upon the bench, and for the last five as the Chief Judge of the
Court. Not only has he won the respect of lawyers and laymen
by his industrious devotion to his duties, the high order of his
judicial work and his unswerving integrity, but it might be said
without exaggeration that a large part of the bar of the city enter-
tains for him a kind of personal regard that is as unusual as it is
creditable to the object of it. At the meeting to be held on Monday this feeling is likely to find expression in a variety of ways,
not least interesting of which will be the presentation to the Chief
Judge of the ivory gavel last used by him in Court, elaborately
mounted in gold and appropriately inscribed.

"The exercises will also illustrate the close connection between
this Court and the other local Courts. The Common Pleas has
exercised certain jurisdiction and functions in probate cases in
common with the Surrogate's Court. It has been the appeal

---
*Hon. Joseph F. Daly.

245

Court for the civil District Courts and the City Courts. Its Judges have been *ex-officio* members of the General Sessions. Judicial representatives of all these tribunals will be heard at the meeting. Sons of its deceased Judges will be among the officers, and eminent lawyers will speak for the bar itself. The consolidation of the Courts under the new Constitution and the resulting abolition of the Common Pleas are generally recognized as necessary judicial reforms. But this meeting and its exercises will furnish the strongest evidence of the high place which the Common Pleas Court and its Judges deserve to hold in popular esteem for the part they have played in the development and advancement of this community."

INDEX.

247

Butler, Benj. F., 31, 203, 209.
Butler, Charles E., 31.
Butler, William Allen, 31, 80, 159, 165–172, 200–204, 208, 209, 222.
Butler, William Allen, Jr., 31.
Byrne, Frank, 133.
Cadwallader, John L., 80, 159.
Cady, Daniel, 146.
Cagger, Peter, 147, 148.
Campbell, Douglass, 91, 139.
Campbell, Samuel, 141.
Campbell, William W., 91.
Cardozo, Albert, 25, 94, 138.
Central Park, 66.
Carter, James C., 80, 159, 229.
Chancery Lane, 186.
Chase, Nelson, 31.
Chase, Salmon P., 122.
Chemical Bank, 105.
Choate, Joseph H., 80, 159.
Choate, William G., 139, 159, 182.
Clarke, John P., 186.
Clark, Horace F., 31.
Clarke, Aaron, 37.
Clarke, T. W., 30.
Cleveland, Grover, 122, 126, 120.
Clinton, Charles A., 30.
Clinton, De Witt, 23, 65, 134, 138, 198.
Clinton, Henry L., 160.
Coke, Sir Edward, 192, 193, 201.
Colden, Cadwallader, 19, 20, 22, 134, 138, 198.
Colden, Cadwallader D., 23.
Columbia College, 61, 68, 70, 75, 81, 86, 97, 125.
Common Council of N. Y., 41.
Conciliation, A Court of, 13, 14.
Cooper, Peter, 132.
Coudert, F. R., 80, 159.
Court, City, 33.
Courts, District, 33, 100.
Court, Mayor's 16, 22, 23, 195.
Court Messenger, 14, 15.
Court of Appeals, 32, 101.

Courts of Chancery, 17, 18, 20, 186, 203.
Court of Errors, 203.
Court of Schout, Burgomaster and Schepens, 9, 12, 194.
Court of Sessions, 16.
Courts, Patroon, 11.
Court, Superior, 25, 32, 33, 66, 69, 80, 95, 109, 205.
Court, Supreme, 16, 19, 21, 22, 24, 29, 31, 32, 33, 34, 68, 69, 89, 94, 97, 98, 103, 104, 109, 114, 120, 129.
Court, U. S. Supreme, 22.
Court, Surrogate's, 33.
Cowdrey, David M., 36, 37.
Cowing, Rufus B., 215–219.
Cumming, James R., 186.
Curtis, William E., 139.
Cutting, F. Brockholst, 30, 36, 37, 38, 39, 135, 138 ,202.
Cram, Henry A., 32.
Da Costa, Charles M., 159.
Daly, Augustin, 106.
Daly, Charles P., 13, 25, 26, 28, 31, 34, 35, 49, 52, 54, 57, 58, 59, 63, 74, 77-82, 83, 88, 115, 133, 138, 139, 155-157, 158, 159, 160, 161, 164, 166, 167, 168, 169, 170, 172, 173, 174, 175-178, 178, 179, 180-182, 183, 185, 189, 190-200, 203, 204, 206, 207, 209, 218, 222, 228, 234, 237.
Daly, Joseph F., 25, 26, 57, 59, 105-108, 113, 126, 132, 157, 182-184, 186, 220, 226, 227-234, 236, 237.
Dartmouth College, 121.
Davenport, James P., 185.
Davies, Henry E., 30, 132.
Davies, Julian T., 30.
Davies, William G., 30.
Davis, Noah, 139, 230.
Depew, Chauncey M., 129.
Devlin, John E., 32.
De Witt, C. J., 31.
De Witt, Edward, 31.

248